Derek Roger spent his professional life in academic research and teaching, mainly at the University of York in the UK, but also at the University of Canterbury in Christchurch, New Zealand, where he lived for 12 years before returning to the UK in 2015. Although he enjoyed a highly successful career in academe, his abiding interest is in practical philosophy, seeking answers to the perennial question of how to act wisely in the world. His search led to many organisations offering answers, but their adherence to particular traditions meant that they remained separate from one another. *Enlightened Living* emerged from Derek's desire to develop an approach which transcends these differences, offering a way of living in the world which is neither spiritual nor esoteric but is instead grounded in the here and now.

Enlightened Living is the result of a path travelled together with my wife, Gwen.

Dr. Derek Roger

Enlightened Living: A Book of Being

Austin Macauley Publishers™
London • Cambridge • New York • Sharjah

A CIP catalogue record for this title is available from the British Library.

ISBN 9781788480154 (Paperback)
ISBN 9781788480161 (Hardback)
ISBN 9781528954129 (ePub e-book)

www.austinmacauley.com

First Published (2019)
Austin Macauley Publishers Ltd
25 Canada Square
Canary Wharf
London
E14 5LQ

I am indebted to the participants in the *Enlightened Living* group meetings, whose questions and observations helped crystallise the approach described in this book.

Chapter 1
Introduction

This is a book about enlightenment, and the subtitle – A Book of Being – tells us a lot about what it means to be enlightened. Everything in the universe is in a process of change, of becoming something different. The time scale for this change may be very long indeed. Our solar system, for example, is around 4.5 billion years old and has about the same length of time to run before the sun expands and then cools, by which time life on earth, as we know it, will long ago have ended. At the other extreme, elementary particles might last for only nanoseconds, but everything has a measure: it comes into existence, lasts for a while and then disappears.

We can hardly comprehend the time scales of the stars or elementary particles. Creatures living on the earth provide an easier way of relating to measure, though their lives too may vary enormously, just a day for mayflies, or hundreds of years for trees. A human measure would be a lifetime, the average 70 to 80 years that we live. If you're reading this now, you must be alive and equally certainly you will one day die. What we are becoming is corpses. The question is, what will you do with the lifetime you have? There aren't any others, just this one, but as human beings, we do have a choice: we can be identified with what is becoming or we can just be. The only time and place you can be is now, so being means being in the present moment. What binds us to the past and the future is *attachments*, and in essence, this is what enlightenment is: freeing ourselves from attachments to things that are here today and gone tomorrow.

What comes and goes are the myriad forms in the universe and Enlightened Living draws a distinction between what passes and what doesn't. What passes makes up the relative world we live in; what doesn't change is consciousness. In truth, there isn't really a distinction between them, since one of the assumptions in this teaching is that everything is a form of consciousness. The difference is that consciousness doesn't change, while everything in the relative world is temporary.

Enlightened Living has had a long gestation, starting when I was a child and wondered, as children do, about the fundamental philosophical question: what am I? That gradually developed into a search for some answers and meandered through various religious and philosophical teachings, all of which were ultimately discarded. Religions all refer to what is supposedly the same God, yet the particular rituals they each cling to create a seeming difference between them that has so often led to hatred and war.

For me, the closest answer came from my long association with a school of philosophy based on a Vedic teaching called Advaita Vedanta, but again there was an adherence to the form of the teaching that necessarily included ideas like reincarnation. There may perhaps be past and future lives, but in the absence of evidence, it is just ritualised faith. Why all this interest in past and future anyway, when all that actually exists in your experience is now? The rest is just thoughts, an imagined life. It is no doubt comforting to think that if you don't quite get it right this time you'll have another chance, or that if you do get it right you'll go to a blissful place called heaven; it probably also keeps people behaving more or less appropriately if straying from the path might lead to being born again as a poisonous worm, or going to hell!

Perhaps the simplest way to put the issue to rest is to refer to an expert. Ramana Maharshi is recognised as one of the foremost Vedic teachers of the last century, but when asked whether reincarnation was true his surprising answer was:

"Reincarnation exists only so long as there is ignorance. There is really no reincarnation at all, either now or before. Nor will there be any hereafter. This is the truth."

His interlocutor persists, asking whether yogis can know their past lives and his further answer is equally forthright:

"Do you know the present life that you wish to know the past? Find the present, the rest will follow."

(Godman (Ed): *Be as You Are: The Teachings of Sri Ramana Maharshi*)

The present moment, now, is all that there is, so any concerns about the imagined past or future are just that: imagined. A contemporary perspective that echoes Ramana Maharshi is provided by Eckhart Tolle:

"You will observe that the future is usually imagined as either better or worse than the present. If the imagined future is better, it gives you hope or pleasurable anticipation. If it is worse, it creates anxiety. Both are illusory. Through self-observation, more presence comes into your life automatically. The moment you realise you are not present, you are present. Whenever you are able to observe your mind, you are no longer trapped in it."

(Eckhart Tolle: *Practising the Power of Now*)

Mark Twain noted that some of the worst things in his life never happened. Indulging in hope or misery serves no useful purpose and since now is all that actually exists, any practice towards enlightenment can only be done now. When that connection is made, what also becomes clear is that there was nothing to work towards and nothing to be sought. Enlightenment is available at all times, now, without having to go somewhere to find it. As we shall discover, all that's required is surrender, taking oneself out of the picture.

What Ramana Maharshi means by ignorance in the quote above isn't our ordinary sense of stupidity. It means to ignore and what is ignored is consciousness. What exists permanently is absolute consciousness. Ignoring it leaves you with only temporary forms, which binds or attaches you to what is temporary and passing. The effect of attachment is seen in the obsessive longing for something you want and grief when it passes.

Faith offers comfort – it is comforting to feel that there's a power greater than ourselves to which we can appeal for intercession and it can help equally with accepting things the way they are by attributing them to the will of God. None of these acts of faith has a place in Enlightened Living. The focus in this teaching is on now. Everything is assumed to be a form of absolute consciousness, but this isn't a being to which you can appeal for intercession. Indeed, consciousness is your own fundamental self, which is why there's no need to appeal to a greater power – you already embody it.

Consciousness is the source of all forms, but since it is the knower it can't be known in an intellectual sense. For a teaching to be useful it has to be based on what we can know and practice using the instruments of body and mind. Although it isn't possible to know consciousness in the ordinary sense, it is possible to know and to work with its reflection through our bodies and minds in the form of *attention*. In the world of forms, attention is what produces everything, from reading and understanding these words to painting the ceiling of the Sistine Chapel. The question is whether it is given intentionally and consciously to things, or is simply an automated and mechanical way of behaving. Consciousness or attention is the theme of Chapter 2, where this will be explored.

Enlightened Living is definitely not 'spiritual' in the conventional sense, but it is not anti-religious. Many people find great comfort in religion, and it isn't the place of this book to call their beliefs into question. The problem is that the forms the various religions and philosophies have taken have often distorted the original message. It is possible to find statements that do represent the common truth that is at the heart of these religions and teachings and quotations from a number of sources will be used to illuminate this 'perennial philosophy'. The sources include mainly Buddhist, Vedic and Christian teachings but extend to writers like William Shakespeare and Mark Twain. Using a variety of texts helps to dissociate Enlightened Living from any one particular teaching and avoids creating yet another set of rituals and dogmas.

Enlightened Living is also not mystical. Mystical teachings have a long history but flourished strongly in Europe during the late 19th and early 20th centuries. They are all to a greater or lesser degree esoteric, describing a hidden knowledge revealed to initiates by mystics who claim to have access to sources of knowledge unavailable to ordinary mortals. One reason for the surge in mystical beliefs may have been a reaction to the erosion of religious beliefs, which were challenged by the rationality of evolutionary theory and other significant advances in science that occurred during this period of history.

Some of these advances, such as quantum physics, are certainly mysterious. This has led to spurious attempts to blur the distinction between spirituality and science, but they are quite distinct. No matter how mysterious it may seem, the relative world remains subject to the laws of science: physics, chemistry, biology and mathematics. There is relative and there is absolute and the province of science is the former – science is about discovering how the laws of the relative world work. Some scientists, early and modern, have nonetheless been deeply religious and are comfortable with having faith. Examining what they say about it suggests that they make a distinction between the laws of matter that they are seeking in their scientific endeavours and the laws of what they might call God and there is a clear understanding that science is not absolute.

Science is a cumulative process, and the laws governing the physical world are by no means fully understood. In the singularities thought to be at the centre of black holes the ordinary laws governing time and space may no longer apply, and physicists can only speculate about what a singularity might be like. However, speculation based on known laws should not be confused with magical thinking, which is the attribution of powers based on faith in the absence of evidence. Enlightenment is not a science and consciousness itself is not subject to ordinary examination, but as we shall see, the expression of consciousness as attention or awareness can be known and used to observe attachments and to surrender them in our daily lives. The world is a mysterious enough place as it is without adding esoteric magic to it, but we seem endlessly willing to suspend reason and logic. By contrast, the aim is to keep this Enlightened Living teaching free of ritualised forms and esoteric ideas.

What will be offered is not prescriptive since what is needed at any given moment can only be known in that moment. Enlightened Living is more of a signpost than a prescription and hence one of the principles is that the word 'teaching' should be treated with caution. It implies that there is a teacher and the idea of having a teacher implies in turn that there is someone who is all-wise imparting knowledge. In Enlightened Living, there is no 'guru', just signposts to enlightenment from the perspective of this teaching for you to discover and practice yourself. Attributing greater awareness to someone else is a mistake since no one has any more consciousness than anyone else. It also leads to worship and idolatry, with a guru substituting for God. This doesn't help either the teacher or those being taught and there are many examples of teachers being seduced by the adulation they receive or being found also to have attachments. Of course, they do – enlightenment isn't once and for all. Shantanand Saraswati described it accurately: enlightenment requires constant vigilance.

The only guide you need is an aspect of mind called *discriminating mind*, which will be discussed with other aspects of mind in Chapter 3. We all possess discriminating mind, but it does become clouded and obscured by attachments. By surrendering attachments it can function as it should, distinguishing between things in the relative world, but more importantly knowing the difference between what is real and true and what is not.

Words like 'reality' and 'truth' are the source of much philosophical dispute and argument; from the perspective of Enlightened Living, true and real means what is absolute and unchanging. This doesn't make the relative world an illusion – it definitely exists, which you can test for yourself by running into a wall! What distinguishes the forms from consciousness is that they are temporary rather than unchanging. You don't need a guru to discover this, since you already know it, however much it might be obscured by attachments.

The real difficulty with the idea of a guru is that it becomes personalised: 'my guru'. Devotees who imagine that enlightenment will somehow leach into them by mere proximity to a teacher have forgotten that they have to do the surrendering. Having a guru can just be a way of avoiding doing anything at all. As Ramana Maharshi said, 'Liberation is not anywhere outside you. It is only within' (*Be as You Are – The Teachings of Sri Ramana Maharshi*). He did suggest that a guru was helpful, but in order to provide a direction and the difficulty we face is finding a path that will lead us out of the jungle of attachments rather than just providing yet more ideas to become attached to.

There are many groups and organisations offering a way to enlightenment and the danger is becoming a kind of philosophical groupie, hopping from the one to another in search of truth. It might well be that the path on offer doesn't suit your particular conditioning, which will throw up obstacles even if the teaching is sound. On the other hand, you might be successively dissatisfied because none of the paths fits with your attachment to how you think things should be done! Here again discriminating mind comes to our aid. Imagine you've arrived at the train station and want to take a taxi home. Outside in the rank are many taxis; the drivers might each take different routes to your home, but as long as they get there, the relevant question is whether you're comfortable with the route they've taken – in other words, does the path suit your particular nature or conditioning? If it doesn't, you're not likely to practice it. If the driver keeps getting lost, that's the time to find another taxi.

However, speaking of a 'route' to enlightenment can be misleading. The view taken of enlightenment in this book is that it doesn't require either a search or a struggle. Talk of going on spiritual journeys suggests that the truth is to be found somewhere else, but it is in fact always available to you if you're prepared to avail yourself of it – it doesn't have to be sought. It will also not be found through suffering. Suffering comes from attachment to things in the relative world and to induce suffering by wearing a hair shirt will only create more attachment and more suffering. Unfortunately, this is just one of the more conventional ways of describing the torture we unnecessarily inflict on ourselves – there are innumerable more subtle ways that attachments are formed!

The way out of suffering is *surrender*, which is the theme of Chapter 8. What is surrendered is the attachment to one or another form, which is what ego is. We will be defining ego more precisely later in the chapter, but when the illusory attachment is surrendered, consciousness is liberated from the bondage of ego. This is enlightenment, which is everyone's birth right. Probably all of us have experienced enlightenment, if only fleetingly and the real challenge is to be able to live as continuously as possible in the light of consciousness. One way that this principle is expressed is being *in* the world but at the same time not *of* the world – in other words, not separating yourself from the world, but not being at the mercy of what it brings.

Detachment or equanimity allows you to be in the world but not of it and what is meant by detachment is the same as the Buddhist notion of non-attachment: not being attached or identified with some passing form, be it a material object or a thought. A common misconception about detachment is that it is somehow cold or unfeeling, but paradoxically, as we shall see in Chapter 9, both detachment and love are simultaneously the qualities of enlightenment.

This introductory chapter outlines the basic principles on which Enlightened Living is based, the first of which is that there are separate forms in the relative world, but that the source of all forms is a single consciousness. One of these separate forms is the very one that is reading these words, the one we each call 'me'. This form is what we usually think we are and in one sense it is the unique physical form together with the unique collection of conditioned ways of behaving that makes each one of us distinct. However, this difference and separation of forms applies only in the relative world; all forms are passing, relative states of consciousness. To distinguish between these two 'selves', throughout this book we will use the well-established convention of referring to the form as *self* and the consciousness that it unchangeably is, as *Self*. Enlightenment is not about denying the existence of the separate forms but being able to acknowledge at the same time that they are separate forms of an indivisible consciousness. This is what is meant by 'seeing the Self in others'. It is impossible actually to see consciousness – what is seen is its reflection through the form, as attention. All forms are forms of the same Self and seeing the world in this way is how unity replaces separateness.

Being both a form and the source of the form leads to a paradox, which is that we use the form to dispense with the attachments to the form, sometimes expressed in the adage of using a thorn to remove a thorn. However we describe it, enlightenment remains paradoxical, but we will endeavour in this book to show that the practice of it is in essence very simple – it is important to not get bogged down in intellectual debate. The instruments available to us for bringing about enlightenment are body and mind. What the body brings to the enterprise are the senses and to use the senses we need only connect with them. The simplest way to be in the present is to connect with any of your senses since they only operate in the present – nobody can hear something that happened yesterday or see something that might happen tomorrow. The 'work' of enlightenment is observation and what is observed is mind, or rather the conditioning and the attachments that are held in the mind. Mind is the reflector of consciousness into the form and is described in Chapter 3.

Although there is no journey to be undertaken to enlightenment it can be represented as a series of steps, and the first of these is to wake up from the dream of ignorance. Ordinary life is lived mostly in a dream, creating stories that will all have ego as the central character. Just like the dreams we have when we're asleep at night, these imaginings seem real until we wake up and recognise that they are just stories. Once we are awake we're in a position to take the next step which is to observe what is happening in the mind. You might say that the mind is the observer, so what's observing what? This is a paradox that we'll return to in Chapter 3, but all we need to acknowledge now is that you can be aware of the thought-stories running in your mind. Since you can't be what you observe, they are being seen from an objective, detached perspective and we then have a choice: to continue to entertain the story by feeding it with consciousness or to take the step of surrendering it. This is letting go – allowing the insubstantial thought to pass, instead of latching onto it and the simplest way to do it is to come back to now by connecting with your senses.

Enlightenment is simple, but you might justifiably say 'easier said than done'! It is simple but not easy, especially the final step of surrendering. This is hardly surprising – we treasure the stories we create, to the point of addiction to them. Discriminating mind needs to be as clear as we can make it so that the thoughts can be seen for what they are; we can then distinguish between useful thinking and the attachments that need to be surrendered. It is also true that the most difficult part is the *thought* of letting go, rather than letting go itself – when it happens, it seems effortless.

Surrendering attachments to what we are not leads to discovering what we are. Discovery doesn't mean finding something brand new, it means taking the cover off; discovering what is already there but not seen. The knowledge we need is available to us but much of the time we just don't see clearly, a state described in the Bible as seeing 'through a glass darkly'. It's a bit like a pond in which you stir up all the sediment – everything becomes dim and opaque. When the sediment settles the water becomes crystal-clear again and just so with the mind. The sediment has accumulated over the lifetime of the pond and the sediment of the mind is the multitude of attachments that have been formed in the search for happiness. What stirs it up is ego. Enlightenment happens when these attachments are surrendered, but we start by allowing the mind to become settled and still. When attachments are surrendered all that is left is the peace of your own Self and it is experienced as true happiness or bliss.

Most people would say they would prefer to be happy than miserable, so what is happiness? A simple example: you're relaxing on a warm summer evening watching the sunset and all is right with the world. You hear a noise but don't pay much attention. You then wander through to make coffee and find that the noise was actually someone taking your car, which is no longer where you parked it outside. Your mind fills with frustration, anger and regret at forgetting to lock the car in the garage. In an instant, all is now wrong with the world and what you experience is misery.

Where's the mistake? Not with the thief, who is also just looking for happiness. The mistake is in the phrase 'my car'. As soon as we're attached to anything it becomes part of us rather than just an instrument for us to use and this applies to anything, even your body and your mind. For the sediment of attachment to settle we need to clarify our minds and to not simply be subject to whatever arises in them. In our little story, suppose you then remember that you'd agreed to lend your car to a friend. They weren't aware you were home so took the car as planned, but you'd got the days muddled. Happiness returns.

What has happened is that you've been thrown between two opposites, happiness and unhappiness and have been unable to maintain detachment. Detachment means being able to keep things in perspective, from a third point that is independent of the opposites that characterise the relative world. Detachment doesn't mean doing nothing! If your car has been stolen, there is a need to notify the appropriate authorities and maybe arrange a lift with a colleague to get to work the next day. There are needs to be met and bodies and minds are the instruments for meeting needs.

The big mistake is for your happiness or unhappiness to depend on something other than your Self, like a car or a thought in your mind. Or a guru! What happens then is that you attribute a value to something which it doesn't possess and this leads to the next principle of this teaching: that *nothing has any intrinsic value or meaning*. 'Thing' means a form, whether it be a human being, an animal, a tree, a rock, a planet, a star or the universe. These are physical things, but it includes subtle things like thoughts. The principle is that all of these forms come into being, exist for a while and then pass. In the case of sentient beings, they're born, they live, they die. If you grieve for someone who has died, who is it you're feeling sorry for? They're dead; it makes no difference to them at all. Of course, there is a sense of loss and this is not to say we should somehow maintain a stiff upper lip and pretend we're not affected, but the truth is that the person you're feeling sorry for is yourself. If someone you know is suffering, what's needed is love, but a rather different love from our ordinary understanding of the word, as we'll see in Chapter 9.

The difficulty with this principle of nothing having any intrinsic meaning or value is that you might then ask, 'what's the point?' The answer compounds the difficulty: there is no point. You're not born with some sort of destiny to be fulfilled and if you create a point, you have something to strive for or be disappointed by if you don't achieve it. Enlightenment isn't achieved. It doesn't require a struggle or a motive, just surrender, including surrender of struggles and motives. So then you might ask, why bother? Don't bother, just be. Fulfilment is meeting the need in the moment. The next question might be whether or not consciousness has a value, but the question is predicated on the relative world where one thing is seen as more valuable than another. Consciousness is absolute and is invaluable – it can't be 'valued', it just is.

Enlightened Living is based on a distinction between the two 'realms' of relative and absolute. The relative world is the one in which we live, the world of forms and things, including the subtle forms of thoughts. All of these forms are relative to one another, bigger, smaller, hotter, cooler, happier, more miserable and for each attribute, there is an opposite one. We use these attributes to describe the forms, but they also become part of the mistaken value we attach to them. We're seldom neutral about things and much of our language casts them into the two extremes of what we either love or hate.

The truth is that happiness is like unhappiness, a passing state of the mind into which emotion has been injected, just as we see in our story about forgetting that you lent your car to a friend. Once you remember the date of the arrangement for your friend to borrow your car, happiness (probably described as relief) returns. You go back to relaxing and watching the sunset, but then the weather suddenly turns and a gale and rain blow in. Misery again! If you attribute your happiness or unhappiness to things like the weather you become bound by them. Sunsets and rain are not joy and misery, they're just sunsets and rain until you attribute a value to them that they don't intrinsically possess.

Attributing value and meaning leads to attachment, either desire for the things we like or aversion to the things we don't. At first, this is simple *conditioning*, such as preferring chocolate ice-cream to vanilla. Conditioning isn't a problem. Conditioning regulates our lives, getting up at a particular time and sleeping at another, instead of just doing things randomly. Conditioning has a mechanical sound to it and in a large degree it is, but you can behave in a conditioned way either being aware of that or not. The real problem arises when we become attached to the fruit of the conditioning. You wake up in the morning feeling comfortable, relaxed and warm and getting up becomes a chore because of attachment to the emotional feelings. Removing the attachment doesn't mean that you'll necessarily just get up when you wake up, but the choice to either get up or to stay in bed needs to be a *mindful* one and the first step is to let go of the idea that staying in bed is slothful and bad while getting up is disciplined and good. Haven't you noticed how proudly people proclaim their early rising? These are just more values being attributed to actions that are, as we shall see, completely empty of value or meaning.

Attachments mean that you're completely subject to what is happening in the world and what's happening in the world is simply following the *law of cause and effect*: what exists at any given moment is an effect of a prior cause and becomes, in turn, the cause of a subsequent effect. In the realm of elementary particles, this no longer applies, but in our ordinary day-to-day experience, that's really all there is to the world, a chain of causes and effects unfolding over time from the past and into the future, involving endless change. The reasons for the causes and effects are irrelevant in Enlightened Living. In 'Food for the Heart', the Buddhist teacher Ajahn Chah said:

"Even though you may be unhappy, it doesn't matter. Is that unhappiness your 'self'? Is there any substance to it? Is it real? Unhappiness is a mere flash of feeling that appears and then vanishes. Happiness is the same. Is there any consistency to happiness? Is it truly an entity? It's simply a feeling that flashes suddenly and is gone... Love flashes up for a moment and then disappears. Where is the consistency in love, hate, resentment? The Buddha knew that because both happiness and unhappiness are unsatisfactory, they have the same value. Once born, they die."

(Ajahn Chah: *Food for the Heart*)

Saying that everything obeys the law of cause and effect shouldn't be mistaken for implying that there is some sort of destiny involved. The idea of destiny is embedded in many teachings and is often extended into lives prior to this one or to follow it. We've already said that reincarnation is a comforting distraction; the truth is that nobody knows what might be next and each of us has only a personal, distorted view of what has happened during the life we've already lived. Destiny is a popular theme of philosophical debate, but in the present, now, it has no relevance.

To be free of the see-saw of opposites, what Enlightened Living suggests is to cultivate *indifference*. Just like the usual response to the word 'detachment', indifference sounds half-dead or not caring at all, but it is quite the contrary. What could be more half-dead than reacting mindlessly with an automatically conditioned or attached response? What indifference actually means is that there is no difference: everything is treated the same, not with misery one minute and ecstasy the next but with a measured acceptance of the way things are and contentment in the moment, whatever that might present. Indifference and detachment are the same and offer the opportunity for the freedom that comes with liberation from attachments.

Being genuinely indifferent introduces another of the principles of Enlightened Living: that *nothing matters*. Saying so will probably evoke the response we talked about earlier: if nothing matters, why bother? It isn't about bothering, which is an effortful action that implies a cost to 'me'. You don't have to bother to be alive; you just are until you die. If there is a 'purpose' to life, it is to ensure that consciousness flows freely, unimpeded by attachments and this means removing your separate self from the scene. Saying that nothing matters follows inevitably from acknowledging that nothing has any intrinsic meaning or value, other than what we attribute to it. If someone close to you dies, you grieve; what about the thousands of others who died at the same time, to whom you give no thought? The meaning that has been attributed is embodied in 'my' friend, 'my' mother or father and the mistake is in the words 'me', 'my' and 'mine'. So does consciousness matter? Just as trying to give it a value constrains it to the relative world, mattering or not mattering doesn't enter into it. Consciousness just is.

Being genuinely free from attachments is not a foreign experience. Most of us have had moments of unattached bliss, where nothing you could have would make you happier and nothing you lost would make you less happy. The freedom and bliss that you experienced then is not just a passing state that depends on what you have or don't have, it is your own Self, reflected in your mind and body as awareness or attention. There is always this bliss, but it gets covered by attachments. We tend to live our lives in ignorance, which, as we've already said, means to ignore. What gets ignored is consciousness, which is what we are. There is a well-known story from the Vedic tradition which illustrates this, about the ten men who cross a raging river and then to make sure everyone has made it across they each count how many of them there are. Each time they only get to nine and fall into despond because one seems to have been lost. The inevitable passing wise man lines them up, counts them off and gets to 10. What each of them had forgotten was to acknowledge themselves, which in the story is a metaphor for forgetting or ignoring the Self.

The attachments we create are to passing states. Only consciousness doesn't change, but because of ignorance most of our actions are egotistical, in the sense that they're devoted to ego. The key to Enlightened Living is to take your separate self out of the frame, to dissolve ego. So what is 'ego'? Attachments are what ego is, identifying what you are with what you are not. A simple, clear illustration of ego is provided by the Sanskrit word for it: *ahankara*. This is a compound of two words, *aham* and *kara*, where kara refers to the forms of the world, including thoughts and feelings. Aham translates as 'I am'. To illustrate the connection, if we drew up a list of what we think we are, it might look something like this:

I am a man/woman
I am a father/mother
I am a daughter/son
I am sad
I am happy
I am a president
I am a beggar
I am beautiful
I am ugly

Each statement has two parts: 'I am' on the left, and what I think I am on the right. Everything on the right-hand side of the list is becoming, changing, here today and gone tomorrow: I might be sad one minute, happy the next; alive one minute, dead the next. On the left-hand side is an unchanging 'I am', with nothing added. In our analogy, 'I am' is *Self.* The changing things like man, woman, happy or sad, are *self.*

The 'I' in 'I am' isn't a separate form but the source of all forms. The mistake is to identify what I am with something passing, like my role, my mood or my body and mind. These changing forms don't disappear when enlightenment dawns, but the difference between what passes and what doesn't pass becomes known. That's when the attachment to the things of the world is dissolved. Ajahn Chah again:

"Whenever we humans hold onto things as being permanent and real, suffering comes immediately. But when we realize the truth of body and mind, suffering is not born. Without attachment, there is no way for suffering to take hold. In all situations, wisdom will arise."

(Ajahn Chah: *Being Dharma*)

The passing states of the mind and body will continue to occur and are neither good nor bad. The trick is to know the difference between what I am and what I am not and to live in the world but not of the world. Understanding begins with being able to know this difference; practising what is known is wisdom and enlightenment and they follow from dissolving our attachments to the things of the world.

One of the greatest aids to enlightenment is *meditation* and meditation is a key principle and practice of Enlightened Living. Meditation is described in detail in Chapter 6 and the emphasis is again on the simplicity of the practice. There are all kinds of mystical connotations attached to meditation, but what it amounts to in essence is sitting comfortably, closing your eyes to exclude the very vivid sense of sight and resting your attention on something that repeats. This might be a word that you repeat in your mind, described as a mantra, but it needn't be a 'special' word. Much is made of the power of mantras, which are often Sanskrit words, but in fact, you can use any word you like. Or you can use breathing as a focus for attention, noting the alternating warm and cool sensations as the breath enters and leaves your body. Many people find breathing the easiest to use because it just keeps repeating and doesn't introduce the associations that come with words.

Whatever device you use, though, the tendency is for the mind to find anything repetitious 'boring' and for it to quickly be distracted by thoughts. This is inevitable and doesn't matter – as you've probably discovered for yourself, there's no point in trying to force thoughts out of your mind. To begin meditating all you need do is to gently let them go by returning attention to the repeating word or to breathing. Eventually, your mind will become still. The effect can be both restful and invigorating, but it is important not to meditate for an effect – it then just turns into something else you need to achieve or feel you're going to personally benefit from.

With practice, meditation can progress into what in Chapter 6 we call 'deep meditation' when even the awareness of a mantra or breathing ceases. There is nothing in the mind; it can't be recalled or described. This deep unity may or may not happen, especially when you first start meditating, but any practice of stilling the mind is helpful for checking the endless, frenetic 'doing' that ego engages in.

Meditation is necessarily a contrived practice, removing sensory stimulation. Repeatedly connecting with the deep stillness that comes with meditation is essential, but you don't remain in a meditative state. What is needed is to allow the stillness that comes with it to inform your everyday actions. Meetings with like-minded people in the name of enlightenment are aimed at erecting the signposts, describing the principles of a teaching so that understanding can be increased. Although this is an important first step, wisdom only comes when the understanding is put into practice. The same is true for reading books about the signposts and there are many available (including this one!). Imagining that reading the book will lead to enlightenment without practice is like thinking that a signpost with London written on it *is* London. You have to follow it to get there, though paradoxically, there isn't really anywhere to go. The only 'journey' is the dedicated practice of the understanding that has been gained.

The practice of Enlightened Living is *observation*, observing mind and body. The emphasis is definitely on mind, since that's where action originates – in a sense, body is a symptom of mind, but mind is very subtle. We all know how our minds can deceive us and the real problem with mind is that, unlike body, it is invisible to anyone else. You can sit in a public place and conjure up the most appalling private thoughts! What complicates observation is the feeling that we ought to change, especially if we don't particularly like what we see.

We find it difficult to just observe because we're so conditioned to having goals to achieve. To some extent this is entirely appropriate in the relative world: if you want to be a doctor or a lawyer you must first complete a long course of study. The problem is that we apply the same principle to everything, including liberation. No qualification is required for enlightenment. Yet another paradox: enlightenment follows from *not* doing. This is expressed in the Vedic tradition as, 'In truth, I do nothing at all'. This doesn't mean that actions cease, but rather that the actions are performed by body and mind, observed as it were from the indifferent Self. It is also described as being able to surrender the fruit of the action, in other words doing something, not for an end but simply as an end in itself, because there is a need for it to be done.

An illustrative example that most of us will have experienced is someone begging for money, which offers an invaluable opportunity for observation and practice. What arises in your mind? Pity at their predicament perhaps, or the suspicion that they'll just use the money for drugs or alcohol? You might cross the street to avoid having to walk past them, or you might make sure you have change on you to give to any beggars you meet. Given all of the options, what should you do? Enlightened Living is not prescriptive, so the answer is that it depends. Do have enough money to give? Maybe not, though paradoxically poorer people are more likely to make charitable donations than those who are richer. Observation doesn't end there: if you do give, do you experience a warm glow of being a charitable giver? You've separated yourself from those you see as hard-hearted for not giving and you've attributed value and meaning where there isn't any. That's claiming the fruit of the action and from the perspective of this teaching is as much an attachment as crossing the street to avoid a beggar. Acting with attachment is informed by ego; knowing how to act in an enlightened way is informed by discriminating mind, which only operates clearly when the mind is still and free from attachments.

The obstacle to clear observation is the addition of anything personal to what's observed. We note an attachment to something, but in our mind, it is me that is attached. In one sense it is, but only while this 'me' remains just ego. Knowing that what is observed is an attachment that has grown from conditioning, but that Self is untouched by the formative desires and aversions, frees us from personalising it. With the benefit of detachment or indifference, it is seen for what it is and that it has no value other than the value we've ended up attributing to it.

From this perspective, our attachments can be seen as the foolish mistakes they are.

So watching this play of the mind is what we need to do, in other words, to be *mindful*. You might be forgiven for thinking that mindfulness was some brand new psychobabble construct, but mindfulness is as old as the first time the question 'what am I?' was asked. The psychological appropriation and interpretation of it is largely misconstrued and since ego is still at the heart of this kind of mindfulness it is not enlightenment. Having a balanced ego is supposedly good mental health, but properly defined as ahankara, ego is a mistake that is the source of all the misery in the world. Enlightened Living is aimed at dissolving it. Psychotherapy is aimed at providing you with a cure for something, which anchors it in achieving a goal. There is no doubt that psychological disturbance makes for a miserable life, but what therapy will do, if it works at all, is to offer a degree of happiness, not liberation. Enlightened Living takes the view that the only thing that needs 'curing' is the mistaken identification of what you are – consciousness – with something you are not. Enlightenment has never emerged from psychotherapy, it happens when ego is altogether dissolved. Ego is no more than a mistaken attachment that obscures what you already are. There isn't a standard you're supposed to achieve and the very act of erecting a standard means that you're striving for something.

The fundamental question that is seldom asked when people talk about mindfulness is: *what is your mind full of*? You may apparently be engaged in a conversation with someone, but all the while thinking about what you're going to do next weekend. Worse still, you may be churning over how angry you feel about something your partner said to you this morning. In other words, your mind is full of thoughts that have nothing to do with the conversation you're supposedly having. In fact, you're not there at all – what you've conjured up in your mind is a virtual reality that you end up inhabiting, instead of giving your attention to what's being said in the present. When you're engaged in these inner conversations and you mislay your phone or the car keys, we describe it as a result of 'absent-mindedness', which is your attention being absent from now. Presence of mind is when your mind is in the present, when all that your mind is full of is unattached attention, and the simplest way to do this is to connect with your senses.

Being present shouldn't be taken to mean that the past and future have either disappeared or don't exist. This is a mistaken idea about being in the now – memories and plans certainly exist, but the point is that they exist only as thoughts. Memories and expectations give form to our conditioning, and they definitely help us make sense of the world. If you were to close your eyes now and just listen to any sounds you could hear, you would recognise most of them. Recognition is memory, so you've been into the past to retrieve the conditioned knowledge of the source of the sound. Knowledge of consequences also ensures that you don't just step on to the road without checking first. What you're doing all the time is drawing on the past and the future to make sense of the world now, and provided the present remains the frame of reference, there isn't a problem. The problem starts when attachment arises: disliking a sound and wishing it would stop, liking another and hoping it will go on forever.

It is possible for past and future to be suspended altogether, in deep sleep and in deep meditation, but just listening, allowing memories and anticipations to arise as they will but without entertaining the attachments that may follow and letting them pass, is effortless and stilling. Striving prohibits enlightenment, so just observe, that's all, with no judgement of what you observe. If there are attachments that bind you in ignorance, you can't dislodge them by struggling to do so. They usually just get stronger, as you've surely found. You can't evict chaotic thoughts, all you can do is observe them, surrender them by taking consciousness from them, and persevere with this practice even if they return. Thoughts are a bit like unwelcome house guests: if you feed them they're likely to stay! What feeds thoughts is attention.

As we shall see in Chapter 7, there is a measure to all forms, and they will only fully be surrendered when their measure is exhausted. Attachments are hard to dislodge. If you expect to observe them and then knock them on the head once and for all, you're likely to end up feeling that you've failed when they keep recurring. Ego is very persistent! There's a simple solution, which is to just keep going and not attribute failure to what unfolds – the road to Damascus happens only in parables. For that matter, don't attribute success to your efforts either. How can we succeed in becoming something we already are? Enlightenment is about discovering this ground of our being, by surrendering attachments.

To summarise the key elements of this teaching:

- Enlightened Living draws a distinction between the relative world of forms and absolute consciousness, although they are not truly separate: the forms are forms of consciousness. The forms include everything, from rocks to thoughts, and they all come into existence, last for a while, and then pass. Everything in the relative world is becoming and changing; consciousness is unchanging.
- Consciousness should not be confused with God – it isn't a power that can be appealed to for intercession. It can't be known at all, in the ordinary way of using our senses, but its reflection through our minds and bodies, as attention, can be known.
- Enlightened living is practical and neither mystical nor esoteric – it doesn't require faith, just the practice of giving attention. Attending is observing, and what we observe is conditioning and attachments.
- Enlightenment isn't a goal you plan for in the future, or try to recall. It only happens now.
- Conditioning can't be removed and doesn't need to be – we would be lost without it – but attachments can be dissolved. Attachments are what ego is: the identification of the consciousness that we are with a passing form. Attachment binds us to the relative and passing states of happiness or unhappiness; enlightenment comes from observing their coming and going without attachment.
- Attachments are fostered by attributing value to the forms of the relative world, but nothing has any intrinsic value – our likes and dislikes are merely attributions that we make to the myriad forms that arise and pass according to the law of cause and effect.

- An individual 'life' has no destiny or purpose other than to allow consciousness to flow freely and not become locked into personal attachments.
- Detachment is indifference to the passing effects, whether or not we like them. The greatest challenge in enlightenment is that the very thing we most love in the world, 'me', needs to be taken out of the picture.
- The sequence of steps towards enlightenment begins with waking up out of the dream of ignorance. Wakefulness is sustained by mindfulness, not mind full of thoughts but mind filled with unattached attention. This state of mind allows the final steps of detachment and surrender to be taken.
- Mindfulness is strengthened by meditation, which is the simple practice of resting attention on something that repeats, without becoming waylaid by distractions. Just bringing the mind to stillness is important, whether or not it leads on to the deep meditation of there being nothing in the mind at all.
- While meditation is an essential practice, it will only be helpful if the stillness of mind is taken back, as it were, into the relative world. The purpose of enlightened living is to be in the world but at the same time not of the world.

For ease of reading, the book is divided into 10 chapters, each one describing a different aspect of the Enlightened Living teaching. Chapter 2 explores *consciousness* and its reflection in our minds and bodies as attention, and Chapter 3 is devoted to *mind.* The fourth chapter expands on *attachment and liberation* from attachment. The misattribution of meaning and value to the things of the world is discussed in Chapter 5, entitled *Emptiness and Fulfilment*. Chapters 6 explores *meditation*, and Chapter 7, *measure and choice*. Chapter 8 is about *emotion and surrender*, and Chapter 9, *love and reason*. The final chapter is about *living in the world*, mindfully.

Chapter 2
Consciousness

The first principle of this teaching is that everything is a form of consciousness, but what is consciousness? The difficulty is that it can't be known directly, in the way that the forms of consciousness can. Enlightened Living is a practical path that eschews mysticism or faith in favour of observation, but it would seem to require an act of faith to accept the existence of consciousness. On the other hand, in the world of astrophysics the gravitational force in black holes is so strong that even light cannot escape from them, so they can't be observed directly. Their existence is inferred from their effects on surrounding objects in space, but nobody doubts their existence. By analogy, while consciousness can't be known directly, we can observe the effect of consciousness reflected in our body and mind as *attention* or *awareness*.

For example, you may be absorbed in thinking about your next holiday, conjuring up a virtual reality in your mind which completely captures your attention. You're oblivious to friends approaching until they greet you. What happens then is that you wake up – quite literally, since the thoughts were just dreams. Your friends might comment that you were 'miles away', which is true – you were on an imagined holiday. It isn't that you were unconsciously thinking about it since consciousness is not absent, but the element of *intention* has been removed. We find ourselves unintentionally absorbed in dream worlds, and are absent-minded; when we wake up our senses come into play, connecting us with the present, and consciousness is available to be given to what is happening now.

You might say that what you're connecting with in the present is equally dream-like. The person you regard as your friend is a form to which you attribute meaning and value based on your perception of them, so in a sense what you meet is a projection of your perceptions onto the form. The question of who they 'really are' could be speculated on endlessly, but what is clear is that our perception of anything is bound to be distorted to some extent by our conditioning. What they really are is consciousness, and it is this knowledge that removes the sense of separation from them or from any other form. Living in an enlightened way doesn't involve theoretical speculation about 'knowing the Self in others', but rather surrendering the view that they are separate because their bodies and minds are different from ours.

To keep this completely practical, let's pursue the example. Suppose the person who greets you is someone you particularly like. The emotional feeling that arises will be quite different from bumping into someone you don't like. Enlightened Living isn't about trying to remove the liking or disliking, but rather not attaching to the feelings when they do arise. In other words, enlightenment takes place within us, not between us: whatever happens between people is an effect, arising from what is done with the perceptions and emotions which capture attention. When that attachment is surrendered, consciousness flows unimpeded.

The difficulty with everything being a form of consciousness is that you, your friend, the space between you, the thoughts in your mind and the attention that flows between you are all forms of consciousness. Our experience of the world is, for the most part, as a separate being from which attention seems to emanate and flow outwards as we give our attention to something, but consciousness is independent of forms – without it, there would be no forms, but consciousness doesn't disappear when the forms pass. Because everything is a form of consciousness, it can nowhere be absent. Here's how Jesus described it, in a 'hidden' gospel that formed part of the ancient manuscripts found at Nag Hamadi:

> (Logion77)
> "I am the Light that is above
> Them all, I am the All,
> The All came forth from Me and the All
> Attained to Me. Cleave a (piece of) wood, I

Am there; lift up a stone and you will
Find me there."

(*The Gospel According to Thomas*)

He certainly didn't mean his separate form when he refers to 'I' and 'Me' – the I and the Me he refers to *are* the All. We can't know what Jesus really thought, but the Christian teaching would give the name God to the All. In Enlightened Living, it would be consciousness, but there is a significant difference: consciousness is not a separate power or creator that you can appeal to with prayer. You, me, Jesus – everything in fact – is the All, since all forms are forms of consciousness.

Another metaphor is to compare consciousness to the sea. The forms in the relative world are like the waves that appear on its surface – each wave is unique, different from every other one, but they're all forms of the undifferentiated sea. However, all that a metaphor provides is another concept, which might fool us into thinking we know what the object of the metaphor is. Consciousness remains a paradox, rather like the Zen metaphor of knowing the sound of one hand clapping: it doesn't have a solution and can't be understood using concepts. Enlightened Living is a practical path to liberation from attachments; we can keep it practical by staying with what we can know, using simple illustrative examples from our experience.

If someone is explaining to you how a particular computer programme works, you give your attention to the words as they're being said, but you'll also be attending to the concept that's building in your mind. Your attention will be moving between what's being said now and the abstract picture, fast enough that it all fits together seamlessly. Once the instruction is completed, you understand how the programme works. The test is then running it yourself, and the combination of abstract learning and practice leads to expertise – in other words, perfected conditioning. This is the equivalent of transforming knowledge into wisdom. However, if some detail is glossed over, your attention may be captured by puzzling about what's been missed. Unless you stop the person at that point while you catch up, you'll miss the next part.

The straightforward process of learning by conditioning is changed by the addition of ego. You may be learning about this computer programme as part of a competitive job interview and any interruption of the learning process can become coloured by emotion: anger that the instructor is going too fast, perhaps, or fear that you'll fail. What's then created is not simple conditioning but attachment. You become identified with the state of mind, and you believe that you're angry or afraid. This is ego: consciousness doesn't get angry or afraid. Emotional states just come and go, but they have a valence we attribute to them, either positive or negative. The passing states are forms of consciousness, but the consciousness that they depend upon has no valence: it is the same consciousness, irrespective of the particular emotion. Consciousness itself is indifferent, but through attachment, it is captured by ego and is coloured by the emotional tone.

Gaining understanding by using metaphors and concepts is an entirely appropriate way of making sense of the relative world but just like learning about computer programmes, to move from understanding to wisdom there has to be practice. The difference is that expertise in the relative world is about accumulating knowledge. Enlightenment is about surrendering any ideas about what you know. Studying, reading, pondering are all necessary starting points and can lead to a greater understanding, but it will remain an abstract understanding until it is practised. You can have all the theoretical ideas about enlightenment at your fingertips but still remain ignorant. In fact, for wisdom to arise, you – in other words, ego – need to be taken out of the picture.

Knowledge of something in the relative world can also set you apart as an admired and respected expert. Admiration and respect are the fuel on which ego feeds, and history tells us that gurus who are admired and respected for their spiritual wisdom sometimes fall into the same trap of ego. This is why there is no room for gurus in Enlightened Living. There are certainly some people who know a lot more about computers than others, but we all have the same capacity for liberation. We could take this further: we are all enlightened, save only for the contamination of the mind by ego. The only step that's required is surrendering attachments. Understanding involves 'thinking mind', and there isn't anything wrong with thinking unless it leads to bolstering ego. Enlightenment might begin with understanding, but wisdom comes from surrendering, not gaining.

Consciousness isn't the same as simply being conscious. You can be conscious in the sense that we ordinarily understand it, walking, talking, eating, but if all of these actions are performed mechanically they're not being done as an intentional, conscious choice. We might just as well be unconscious and we are, in effect, in a state of waking sleep, little different from sleepwalking. To make a conscious choice we need to be in the present, appraising what is in front of us, choosing how to act by using the functions of mind which we will be describing in detail in Chapter 3. This will include drawing on our experience of the past and considering what our actions might lead to in the future, but the frame of reference remains the present. What is needed for understanding is clarity of mind, free from the obscuring effect of attachments.

The habits that have arisen from conditioning can be performed consciously or unconsciously. Your office might be moved from the 4th floor of the building up to the 6th floor, but because of the unconscious exercise of habit, for the next few weeks, you find yourself automatically getting out on the 4th floor until the new habit is established. Or you might remember each time you get into the lift that your office is now on the 6th floor – this is mindfulness in action; it applies as much to ordinary everyday behaviour as it does to seeking enlightenment. Habits are the result of benefiting from either doing or avoiding doing something, and habits can be very useful indeed. If you're in the habit of meditating at a particular time every day you're much more likely to be meditating regularly than someone who does it haphazardly, but even meditation can become an empty habit, regularly sitting down, closing your eyes and thinking about your day for half an hour.

Eating provides an everyday example: during a meal, we may be engaged in conversation with someone, or absorbed in our heads. The food is eaten mechanically, hardly tasted at all because we're disconnected from our senses. We don't need to sit in silence, adopting what we imagine will appear to be enlightened behaviour. This is just posturing. The endeavour is to be present as much as possible, by surrendering attachments, acting naturally in accordance with what is needed in each moment. As Shantanand Saraswati noted, enlightenment needs constant vigilance.

Attention or awareness seems like the beam of a torch that lights things up, though the analogy doesn't have to be a visual one. You might become aware of a bird singing outside, and when listening switches to it you'll be aware of the sound the beam has illuminated. We can also be aware of having had our attention taken away by something but that's always retrospective. Only after we've woken up from being distracted into memories evoked by associations with the birdsong do we realise that we were no longer listening. The fact that attention does get pulled away like this is not in itself a problem. Once you realise you've been distracted by thoughts you've woken up, and the challenge of enlightenment is to remain awake and connected for as long as you can.

The degree to which we're aware can vary enormously. In deep sleep, there is no awareness of anything at all. The mind is completely inactive, as is the body apart from essential processes for maintaining life, and it is relatively difficult to wake someone from deep sleep. We are effectively unconscious, which doesn't mean that consciousness has disappeared or been diminished, we're just not consciously processing anything. The next stage is when we start to dream; we move about and may even talk. When people are dreaming their eyes flicker back and forth under their lids, what's called REM (Rapid Eye Movement) sleep, and dreamers are easier to wake up than when they are in deep sleep. We have a brain mechanism that more or less paralyses us when we dream, preventing us from acting out them out. Everyone dreams, but in another state which only affects some people – sleepwalking – they may engage in surprisingly complicated activities, talking, dressing, even preparing meals. They appear to be awake, but they're on a kind of mechanical auto-pilot.

So what is a dream? A virtual reality conjured from thoughts. A dream might reflect in some way something that's happening in your life at the time, or it might not. Some would claim that dreams reflect hidden psychological processes in a symbolic way that can be interpreted. That seems unlikely, but even if it were true, of what use is it? Supposedly analysing the meaning of dreams has nothing to do with enlightenment. Like realising our attention has been snatched away, knowledge of dreams is also always retrospective: if you have a nightmare you're only aware of it when you wake up and think, 'thank goodness it was only a dream'. A dream is a dream. We need to be more concerned with what it means to be awake.

In each of these successive stages of sleep, from deep sleep to sleepwalking, people become more and more active and articulate; measuring brain activity at each stage reflects the relative level of wakefulness that they represent. What we might assume is that the next stage after sleepwalking is waking up when we engage in the demands of the day, but how awake are we? Earlier we referred to 'waking sleep': a state when we're talking, managing people, doing jobs, but we may be doing everything without conscious intention. When did you last set off to drive somewhere and found yourself at your destination but with little or no recollection of the journey? If you say you've travelled the same route many times before, think again: was it ever actually the same? Was the sun shining? Was it raining? Everything changes all the time, but we drift into waking sleep and think that nothing changes. Familiarity does indeed breed contempt, and since nothing except the present actually exists, this is contempt for life itself.

There will always be some degree of waking sleep. No one is awake all the time and if you don't give your mind something to occupy it, it will go off and find something – it needs to be entertained! So the question isn't so much whether or not there is waking sleep, but how much time we spend in it, apparently awake but in fact operating in a fashion no less automatic than sleepwalking. And what is it that really wakes you up? Take the way that we behave in emergencies, such as an approaching car suddenly swerving into our path. What has happened is unexpected and you need to attend when things are novel. In other words, you need to be in the present, where the novel action is unfolding, which is why people who behave appropriately in emergencies are described as having presence of mind – their minds were in the present.

The appropriate action doesn't always occur, which is one reason why people have accidents. Fortunately, the different functions of mind we describe in Chapter 3 include monitoring what's happening on the road ahead, but unfortunately, the extent to which it does so is a function of the degree to which the mind has become immersed in thoughts about the past or the future. Minds that are completely engaged elsewhere will fail to wake up in time. Many countries have laws against using mobile phones while driving because being engaged in a conversation means that your attention is elsewhere, but what about the conversation you're having in your head? This can't be controlled by legislation; it only ends when you wake up and come into the present. Once in the present, what is held in the mind is available for observation.

"Mindfulness is knowing, or presence of mind. What am I thinking right now? What am I doing? What am I carrying around with me? We observe like this, we are aware of how we are living. Practicing like this, wisdom can arise."

(Ajahn Chah: *Food for the Heart*)

You might also say you 'came to your senses', an aphorism which describes one of the key practises in Enlightened Living: connecting with your senses. Doing so connects you directly with the present and provides the opportunity for regaining perspective:

"Come back now to your sober senses; recall your true self; awake from slumber and recognise that they were only dreams that troubled you; and as you looked on them, so look now on what meets your waking eyes."

(Marcus Aurelius: *Meditations*, Book 6)

As we pointed out in Chapter 1, all of our senses only operate in the present. You can imagine what you saw yesterday or what you might see tomorrow, but these are just thoughts. All that actually exists is now; certainly, during emergencies, there isn't time to try to recall the account you read about the way someone responded in a similar situation. What you become aware of in the present may still, to a degree, be passing through the distorting lens of conditioning and attachments, so waking up needs to be followed by surrendering the attachments to allow you to see clearly. Having our minds clouded by the attachments of ego is what is meant by 'seeing through a glass darkly' in *1 Corinthians*, and one of the miracles attributed to Jesus was returning sight to the blind. Perhaps he did, but Enlightened

Living doesn't entertain miracles; it seems more likely that the sight they gained was being able to see clearly, unimpeded by ego.

What actually happens when we wake up depends on the need. Waking up to an emergency will result in action, accompanied by significant biochemical changes in our bodies, but interestingly, survivors who act appropriately in emergencies will often report feeling no fear at the time. This will seldom be experienced as an intentional process of observing the fear and surrendering it, but the attachment to the emotion clearly hasn't formed. The way these people acted would have involved some degree of conditioning, but since the circumstance is novel they will be responding almost entirely to what is presented in the moment. There will certainly be no attachments – the anxiety about what might have happened only occurs to them afterwards.

This is mindful action, when consciousness flows unimpeded to meet the need, but we don't need to be in an emergency to be mindful. Just pose the question: right now, where is your attention? It might have wandered off half-way down the page and become absorbed in some plan or recollection. Once you wake up, you can intentionally give your attention again to the words. Taking this a step further, in meditation, attention is given to something that repeats, like breathing. If attention is steadfastly brought back to breathing each time it wanders, eventually the mind settles and is aware of nothing except breathing. Eventually, the awareness of breathing disappears too, and all that the mind is full of is consciousness with no attachments at all. As we'll see in Chapter 6, since there is no object of awareness it isn't possible to describe deep meditation but what remains afterwards is an experience of bliss – not *my* bliss, but the bliss described as the 'peace that passes understanding'. This isn't the same as happiness, which is dependent on something either outside of yourself or a pleasant thought in your mind. What we're calling 'bliss' is an unattached contentment which defies analysis; indeed, it will evaporate the instant you try to conceptualise it.

Here's a simple way of getting a glimpse of consciousness: read through this paragraph first so you know what you need to do, then close your eyes for a moment. Allow any tension held in your body to dissolve, and make sure you can breathe comfortably and easily. Then, using consciousness reflecting through your mind as awareness, rest that awareness on any sound you can hear. Initially, conditioning will be activated and you'll recognise the sound, probably forming a picture of it in your mind while anticipating the sound that's likely to follow. Try gradually to not anticipate sounds or to hold on to the sounds you can hear – let go of the thoughts and pictures that the sounds evoke. If you become distracted, as soon you as you realise that has happened, bring your attention back to the sounds. Attention will be drawn into the stories we create in our minds, and you can only realise your attention has been taken away into thoughts after it has happened. These thoughts are just dreams and like any dream, we're only aware we were dreaming when we wake up. Each time you wake up from the dream that's been created in your mind, you're able to reconnect your attention with the sense of listening, so just return your attention back to the sounds.

Consider what happened when you tried the exercise. Did your mind continue churning over something that's preoccupying you at the moment, without a break? Or, did you find your mind moving between unattached listening and the evoked conditioning and attachments? Or were you able to let go quite quickly and just rest your attention on the sounds? It would be a mistake to rank order these three different possibilities, with the third alternative being the best and the first one the worst: we're then making judgements and attributing values to our experiences. The aim of the exercise is, of course, to still the mind and just listen without distraction, but if that doesn't work we're able to realise, in practice, just how strongly these ideas can capture us. Whatever happens, happens; therefore, any attempt at practice is instructive.

The listening exercise shows clearly the nature of attention, as well as revealing both conditioning and attachment. When you hear a sound you've heard before, your mind will quite naturally link what you can hear to your previous association with the sound. This is conditioning; it can easily be acknowledged and let go by just attending again to the sound. If it is a new sound your mind will start to cast about to make the association. We're comfortable with things that are familiar and we use our senses and our minds all the time to understand the world around us; if you opened your eyes and found the source of the sound you would then have formed another conditioned association that you can call upon next time you hear that sound.

It is certainly more difficult to acknowledge and let go of novel sounds, but you can do so by not trying to control everything and just listening. Much more difficult, however, is surrendering attachments. For example, the sound may evoke an emotional entanglement that's preoccupying you and you may end up experiencing the whole gamut of emotions: anger to fear to jealousy. You may not even need a sense impression like a sound to provoke the emotional preoccupation: as if from nowhere, you conjure up an entire world in the mind, replaying from your perspective the things that have happened and most probably recasting them so that you end up the all-suffering martyr or the all-conquering hero. The imagined martyrs and heroes are ego, which is what attachment is.

When you see this for what it is and connect your attention again with just listening, the shadow-play of thoughts evaporates. It never existed in the first place. What is interesting about it, though, is that while the emotions change and fluctuate, attention doesn't – you give the same attention to all of these varying states of the mind and they're lit up as you give them attention. As we've said, attention is neutral – it doesn't have an emotional tone. The emotions are added by conditioning, which may then be transformed into ego by attachments. Earlier in the chapter, we used the analogy of a torch beam, which is neutral; what it lights up provokes the conditioned response. Ramana Maharshi uses a cinema screen to illustrate:

"On that screen you see the entire show, and for all appearances the pictures are real. But go and try to take hold of them. What do you take hold of? Merely the screen on which the pictures appeared. After the show, the pictures disappear, what remains? The screen again.

So with the Self. That alone exists, the pictures come and go. If you hold on to the Self, you will not be deluded by the appearance of the pictures. Nor does it matter if the pictures appear and disappear.

You may be deceived into believing that a piece of rope is a snake. While you imagine the rope is a snake, you cannot see the rope as a rope. The non-existent snake becomes real to you, while the real rope seems wholly non-existent."

(Godman (Ed): *Be As You Are – The Teachings of Ramana Maharshi*)

It is important to remember that these are all just metaphors, and metaphors are not reality – when we get drawn into speculating about what the screen is, what the projector is, etc., the purpose of using the metaphor is lost. They provide an aid for understanding and shouldn't be taken too literally, just as the model of an atom has a nucleus at the centre with electrons circling round it like planets; the reality is much more subtle.

Being as practical as we can, what happens when you 'listen'? All around us, sounds are being generated and they create a widening ripple of waves. The energy is transferred to what they encounter, including eardrums, which then vibrate. The energy of the vibration is transferred to fine hairs, lining your inner ear, and the movement of these hairs transmits the energy as an electrical signal which is interpreted by the brain. What the brain uses for this interpretation is conditioning. With sounds that are around us all the time, we hardly even register them, which is why when you do close your eyes and become still, you're suddenly aware of what seems a very loud tick from a clock. When the sound is novel we explore until the source is known; it is then added to the catalogue of conditioning.

Allowing listening to occur will include the conditioned response, but without taking the fateful next step of entertaining the thoughts that accompany it and becoming part of the story. If we're asked to listen to something, ego can so easily sneak in under the guise of conditioning, using consciousness to create stories about the sound: when we last heard it, the emotions that it evokes, even empty philosophical debates about whether a tree falling in the forest makes a sound if there's nobody there to hear it! Of course it does. Once attention has been taken away like this we're not allowing listening anymore. The conditioning won't stop. There will still be the recognition of what's heard, but without ego laying siege to it. We can listen with or without the commentary from ego, and what's needed to just allow listening is surrender; as we'll see in Chapter 8.

Just allowing listening to occur in this way, without trying to manipulate it or control it, leads to stillness of mind. The world doesn't stop, birds sing and traffic continues but instead of being involved in it, the activity is observed from a still point. We seldom allow our minds to become still, and this is a significant step towards enlightenment.

Now let's take it a step further. When we close our eyes and listen, is there just listening, or is there the sense of someone – 'me' – listening? If there is just listening, the sounds continue to be registered, but it is all kept under observation and that observation isn't personal. A way to understand this is not 'to listen', but 'to allow listening'. In other words, to not think we have to perform an act of listening and instead just letting it happen, as it will do regardless of how we interpret it.

To allow the listener to disappear while just closing our eyes and listening is difficult, because this 'me' character from whom we tend to take our perspective is usually lurking in there, however subtly. This is how meditation often starts, with attention being caught up in thoughts. If it is gently brought back to the repeating technique every time it does so, your mind eventually settles and there is just a mantra or breathing. With continued practice the awareness of these too can disappear: they've served their purpose and we enter the deep meditation we will discuss in Chapter 6. When the meditation period ends, the conditioning reasserts itself but there is a kind of echo of stillness left behind, and conditioning can more easily be observed without transforming it into attachment.

It is this stillness of mind in meditation that is taken back, as it were, into the relative world of activity. The effects of waking up are clear in emergencies, but the principle is no different in ordinary day-to-day activity: you can do anything with either a still or an agitated mind, with consciousness either free or attached. Emergencies are certainly novel and unexpected, but so too is everyday life. Things may appear to be the same but they never are; the trap is in deciding that they are the same and taking them for granted, even becoming bored. Boredom is a decision, but one which is based on a mistake and is hardly a conscious decision. For almost any activity you can think of, there will be some who describe it as boring and others who are engrossed by it. What this tells you is that boredom is not inherent in anything in the world.

Repetitious tasks are just that, repetitious, not intrinsically boring. We need to know when we're entertaining the idea of being bored, and what's required is observation. Watch what's running through your mind. Thoughts won't stop and trying to fight against them and keep on applying yourself to repetitious tasks will only lead to doing them less well. Rather than working against ego, dissolve it: take a lot of breaks to refresh your mind, turning your attention outwards and reconnecting with your senses.

Drawing distinctions between different states of being awake or asleep shouldn't be misinterpreted as implying that consciousness has somehow progressively faded away and eventually disappeared in deep sleep. There may no longer be awareness of things in the world, but consciousness itself is never absent. Ramana Maharshi expressed this simply and succinctly:

"We may roughly put it like this. Existence or consciousness is the only reality. Consciousness plus waking, we call waking. Consciousness plus sleep, we call sleep. Consciousness plus dream, we call dream."

(Godman (Ed): *Be as You Are – The Teachings of Ramana Maharshi*)

The key is to use consciousness to observe what's happening in body and mind, but especially in mind, which is where actions start. One of the stories told to illustrate attention is about the arrow-maker so engrossed in his work that he doesn't even notice the passing noisy wedding procession. In a sense, the arrow-maker has become one with the arrow, though the analogy is a limited one – the arrow-maker is still making an arrow. The way the mind acts in the emergencies that we talked about earlier is the opposite, being completely connected with everything that is happening simultaneously in the world around us. Neither of these states of the mind is preferable to the other, they're just different. In one case, being engrossed in something, attention is concentrated on a single point. This is what concentration means – not diluted. In the other, attention is open and alert to all that is changing. Neither of them is the same as deep meditation, but they represent the way that actions unfold while being observed from a still point.

A common expression of the way attention is used is in sport, where beginners have to think about every action until it is perfected. Perfecting actions is what conditioning is. Perfected conditioning frees the mind to give attention to the present, and many sportsmen and women will use precisely this terminology – the American golfer Tiger Woods, it seems, often speaks about being in the moment. This is mindful action, and it is where meditation usually begins, becoming still, resting attention on just a mantra or breathing, but it is not the same as deep meditation when activity ceases. Performing perfected actions is often described as being 'meditative', but you can't be in deep meditation and play golf at the same time!

The real difference, though, between enlightenment and mindfulness while engaged in activities is that activities have a purpose. Enlightenment doesn't and for as long as we practice mindfulness and meditation to improve ourselves or achieve something, enlightenment will escape us. We're conditioned to thinking that everything we do needs to have some sort of outcome, but there is nothing to be gained from enlightenment – it has no point. And we needn't stop there. People want to know what's the point of their life, and there isn't one. Why should a temporary form, subject to whatever arises in the unfolding of the law of cause and effect, have any point? There is no destiny, nothing ordained. Destiny and purpose are both locked in time, in the past and the future, but all that actually exists is now. You can, of course, be interested in enlightenment and play golf, but golf won't lead to enlightenment. Pastimes are just that, they pass the time between meditations; the question is whether they are performed consciously or asleep.

You can demonstrate the difference between open and focused attention for yourself, by concentrating now on something in front of you, one word on the page, for example. Continue to keep attention on just that one word for a bit; then at the same time, be aware of all the other words surrounding it. Then open further, to take in all of the room around you in your peripheral vision. Attention is constantly fluctuating in this way and is responding to the need. Since you can give your attention to only one novel thing at a time, nobody can actually 'multitask'. People described as multitaskers are very skilled, but what they're skilled at is moving attention between things so fast they appear to be attending to more than one thing at a time. Unfortunately, in the process of attending to things the needs of ego will all too often intervene! When you gave attention to just the one word on the page, how long did it remain there? And when you opened up the perspective to take in the rest of the room, what thoughts came in to distract you?

The distractions are triggered by conditioned responses, like wondering what's the point of just looking at this one word, or noticing the dust on the floor when you open your attention and in the next moment, finding yourself imagining vacuuming it up. The awareness of the dust is one thing, creating a story around it is another, and consider for a moment the central character on whom all of these stories are centred: the 'me' who always has to do the cleaning because nobody else will, what will visitors think of me if they notice all the dust, and so on. This is ego, the mistaken identification of what we are with what we're not. If there's dust on the floor, allow discriminating mind to decide whether or not this is the time to vacuum it, then vacuum it or not. But just vacuum it or not, without the melodrama of thinking that some else should be helping. You might say this is a recipe for being put upon, but who's being put upon? Ego.

Our ordinary sense of attention is that it is personal as 'my' attention beaming out from me and in one sense that's true: you ask someone to pay attention to something you're describing, and they shift the beam onto the topic, but the point is that the attention you're giving and the attention the other person is giving are the same. What differs is the interpretation made of what's being described or the emotion that becomes attributed to it, arising from our individual conditioning. The difficulty in trying to grasp this is that since all forms are forms of consciousness, the form that constitutes the other person, the form that you are, the object of attention and the attention itself must all be the same consciousness. However, before wandering off into philosophical thickets here is part of a quote from the Buddhist teacher Ajahn Chah:

"And yet this knowing mind is also the mind, so who's observing the mind? Such ideas can make you extremely confused. The mind is one thing, the knowing another... That which knows these things is what is meant by the 'knowing'... The mind is that which thinks and gets entangled in emotions, one after the other."

(Ajahn Chah – *Food for the Heart*)

In Enlightened Living, we would call the 'knower' discriminating mind, which will encounter the moods and emotions triggered by conditioning but can see them for what they are, passing states. Then there is ego, which is the entanglement in the emotions that accompany the conditioning. 'Knowing' here means just witnessing, and that's what consciousness does – it is an indifferent witness.

Consciousness is sometimes described as energy, but this a metaphor that should be used cautiously. Consciousness has no form of itself but it manifests as different forms. Giving attention is like allowing consciousness to light up or energise some particular object or thought, but allowing isn't 'doing'. It is more like not doing – just getting yourself out of the way by dissolving the attachments that make us appear separate. There may be an emotional response to the object or thought, but consciousness is unaffected by the emotion. You can't observe consciousness but you can observe the forms it takes, and from a practical perspective this is all that this teaching is advocating: observe without comment and act in accordance with what is perceived to be needed. This might mean not taking any particular action; it depends on what is observed, but knowing what to do does require that it is as little tainted by ego as possible. What is needed to act in this way is that discriminating mind is as clear as it can be.

You might have a habitually negative view of someone, conditioned by them speaking impulsively about things and offending people. Attachment is formed to the negative view we have, which is no longer impartial. To avoid forming the attachment, we need to accept that the first part of the process will happen: when you encounter that particular person again the conditioned response will most likely be triggered. However, if you see the response rising in your mind, that's the point at which things can take an entirely different course: instead of feeding the thought with inner comments like 'here we go again, just what I would have expected', etc., you see that this person is, in fact, the same consciousness as yourself that has been conditioned in a particular way that may be different from your own conditioning. That means they're not like you – each form is unique – and most of what we dislike about others is that they're not like us!

Allowing the incessant judgements to recede like this is useful and usefulness is what restricts it to the relative world. The outcome is that there is less harm done, but taking it further, what can actually arise is love. Not attached love, but rather the realisation of unity, despite the differences in conditioning. The attention we lavish on those we love is often a form of attachment, a passing state that arises between two separate beings. In truth, consciousness *is* love, but as we shall see in Chapter 9, the love we're speaking of here is unity – it isn't a temporary state existing between two or more forms. We're always so quick to judge, which is the message in the parable of the woman caught in adultery who the scribes and Pharisees said should be stoned. Instead of taking the side of either the woman or her accusers, Jesus merely invites the person free of sin to cast the first stone:

"And they which heard it, being convicted by their own conscience, went out one by one, beginning at the eldest, even unto the last: and Jesus was left alone, and the woman standing in the midst."

(*John 8:9*)

Their conscience is the discriminating mind which we will describe in Chapter 3, that function of mind which knows what is true and what is not and it can only function properly when lit by clear consciousness. For the accusers of the woman their discriminating minds had been clouded by attachments, which were suspended by Jesus's words: that in truth, there is no separation. Again, an analogy helps: if you take a clear white light and shine it through different coloured filters, it takes on the colours. In other words, it has become conditioned by the filter, but remove the filter and there is only white light. When we 'see through a glass darkly' we're seeing the world filtered through our conditioning, but if we can observe the conditioning for what it is and not become attached to it, consciousness is set free.

We can describe the life of an individual form as beginning at some time in the past, being now, and ending at some time in the future, and the question is what will the life be devoted to between existing now and passing away. You can't not act – even inaction is an action. Our individual forms don't have any intrinsic value or meaning other than that which we attribute to them. Our lives have no purpose other than the goals we set for ourselves in the relative world – the forms just come and go, subject to cause, effect and measure. Ensuring that we don't then fall prey to feelings of pointlessness is the focus of Chapter 5, but let's look at the life of the form you call 'me' from a different perspective: each form is a form of consciousness, which can either be captured and subverted for ego's purposes, or can be allowed to flow freely.

Here's another example of how to practice Enlightened Living. Think back to the last time you happened on a conversation between two people who were assassinating the character of an absent third person. Ego is immediately tempted to add its own little snippet of gossip and to collaborate in the assassination. Doesn't it feel good? And isn't it completely dark ignorance? Just because something feels good doesn't mean it is necessarily ignorant, though it is only ego that feels good or bad about anything. As an alternative, instead of collaborating in the gossip, think of some attribute the absent person possesses that is really admirable and bring that into the conversation instead. You don't need to go preaching about how he or she is a form of the same consciousness – you'd pretty quickly end up with the office appellation of 'really weird' – but introducing something positive will usually stop the gossip dead. Another alternative: just walk away. It isn't any of your business anyway.

There are ways we can act differently in the world, but acknowledging that everything is a form of the same consciousness has to precede actions like the ones we've described above. You don't introduce a positive aspect of the absent person in order to save them from gossip – the gossip, the gossipers, your desire to change the process, are all manifestations of ego. This is why Enlightened Living doesn't prescribe. You can't prescribe a solution for something that hasn't happened, you can only act in the present, according to what is presented and what is needed. Acting in these practical ways we've described is also not about wanting an effect. Even apparently alleviating suffering is an effect, and if you're acting for a purpose you will harvest the fruit of the action and become attached. You can become attached to 'good' works as much as to 'bad', and the key is to be indifferent to both.

Ignorance is devoting the life to ego, and ego is the source of all misery. What has happened is that the pure light of consciousness has been subverted. The way to live in the light of truth is to stop allowing ego to hijack consciousness. In the Nag Hamadi gospel, Jesus sums it up in a single sentence:

> (Logion 42)
> "Become passers-by."
>
> (*The Gospel of Thomas*)

Difficult to practice – we do so want to be famous and to stand out from the crowd that just passing by seems completely alien. To outshine others means that we have to compete for fame. There is nothing wrong with competition, but consider it in the context of sport: we play to win, but if we're only interested in winning we neither enjoy the playing, the winning or the losing: if we do lose we become resentful and downcast, and if we win we're triumphant and crowing. Being a 'good sport' means being indifferent to the outcome, enjoying the game and neither crowing about winning nor resenting defeat. 'Winning' or 'losing' are just passing states and nowhere is that more apparent than in sport!

There are differences in our natures that lead to differences in the ways the lives unfold, some richer, some poorer, but these attributes have no intrinsic value or meaning. The purpose of the life, from the perspective of Enlightened Living, is to take ego out of the picture so that consciousness can flow unimpeded by attachments. What we mean by fame is being known to everyone as 'special' in some way: richer, cleverer, more all-suffering. In other words, separate. At the core of fame and overweening ambition for glory or misery is the belief in being separate. Bodies and minds are all different owing to the conditioning of nature and nurture, but separateness is ego. Surrender being famous; in that way, there is nothing that can contaminate consciousness as it is reflected through mind and into the world to meet the need. That's the only purpose of the individual life.

Chapter 3
Mind

Mind is at the heart of Enlightened Living. What we observe when we're mindful and awake is the way we act in the world, but as we saw in the first chapter, one of the difficulties with the current enthusiasm for mindfulness is that the fundamental question is not asked: what is your mind full of? We were able to answer that in the context of attention, which is the reflection of consciousness through our bodies and minds. It is never absent and never diminished, but problems arise when it is captured by attachments and put to the service of ego. When the attachments that comprise ego are surrendered, consciousness remains, and all that your mind is full of is attention, uncontaminated by ego and available for meeting the need in the present.

All behaviour originates in the mind, so the next question is, what is mind? In trying to define it we face similar problems to those we encountered in trying to define consciousness, but the difference is that mind is part of the relative world – it has a form, manifesting as thought. Thoughts are subtle rather than material, but nonetheless amenable to observation.

There is a common distinction drawn between body and mind, but they can't be separated. If something startles you, information has to have been processed about how potentially threatening it might be. The evaluation of the event occurs as a thought but is immediately translated into bodily action by provoking a cascade of biochemical changes usually described as the 'fight or flight' response. Thus we might regard body as inert, acting only when stimulated by mind. On the other hand, mind is plainly a function of brain, and brain is definitely body! It is also true that what happens in your body feeds back to your mind: if you notice your heart racing, that might trigger feelings of anxiety.

Historically, there have been many attempts to attribute the differences in the ways people think and act to differences in their brains. A century or so ago, phrenologists claimed that different mental faculties could be assessed by measuring the part of the skull thought to overlay that particular part of the brain. These ideas were quickly shown to be pseudoscience, and scanning techniques that have become available in the past few decades offer far more precise ways of relating different kinds of thinking and acting to specific parts of the brain.

However, this doesn't really tell us much about mind in the way it is involved in enlightenment. In this chapter we will describe functions of mind that are not intended to be linked to neuroscience models of the brain – Enlightened Living is essentially a practical teaching, and we're less interested in brain structure than in the way that aspects of mind might be used, either to bind us through attachment or to liberate us. In the interests of avoiding a theoretical philosophical debate, we'll regard mind as being a function of brain. Thinking is what mind does and it is usually tranlated into action, though mind doesn't necessarily involve overt behaviour: you can think while remaining quite still. Thinking doesn't stop, except when you're dead, in deep sleep or in what we describe in Chapter 6 as deep meditation. Although deep sleep and deep meditation are very different from one another, you can't recall anything from either of them because during these times the sense of existing as a separate individual is suspended.

From the perspective of Enlightened Living, the real question is: how steady is your mind? In deep meditation, mind is not so much steady as completely still, so the question of steadiness doesn't arise. When there is mindful concentration on something, mind can become very steady, excluding everything except the object of attention – in Chapter 2 we used the example of the arrow-maker, unaware of the passing wedding procession. In that example, mind is steady while attention is concentrated, but what happens when it isn't concentrated?

Opening attention to the world exposes it to the tumult of the senses and mind can then become very unsteady indeed, subject to the pull this way and that. To live in an enlightened way means being able to maintain a still point from which to observe the movement of mind, even under the onslaught of sense impressions. This is why mindfulness can only be maintained by constant vigilance, watching the antics of the mind without becoming involved in them. Mind will continue to move, but instead of being dragged along with it, the movement to and fro is watched with indifference. There is much debate about free will and choice, but from the perspective of this teaching, the real choice is whether or not you become involved in the dramas.

Describing mind in this way makes it seem like a wayward child, constantly having to be controlled. Vigilance then becomes an effortful process, but it is just watching. You can test this for yourself by just listening, noting the sounds as they arise as well as the conditioned associations they trigger, but without becoming involved in them – more a resting of attention on the sense impressions and thoughts, rather than a participatory and active listening. However, the idea of observing your mind can be confusing: since mind is the instrument being used to make the observation, what's observing what? We considered this question briefly in Chapter 2 and we used part of a quote from Ajahn Chah to provide a way of resolving the paradox. Here's a fuller version of the quote:

"And yet this knowing mind is also the mind, so who's observing the mind? Such ideas can make you extremely confused. The mind is one thing, the knowing another, and yet the knowing originates in this very same mind. What does it mean to know the mind? What's it like to encounter moods and emotions? What's it like to be without any defiled emotions whatsoever? That which knows these things is what is meant by the 'knowing'... The mind is that which thinks and gets entangled in emotions, one after the other... Whatever direction it strays in, maintain a watchful eye."

(Ajahn Chah: *Food for the Heart*)

Ajahn Chah distinguishes clearly between the still point of the knowing mind and the entanglement in moods and emotions. We've considered the idea of consciousness reflected as attention in the mind that seems to emanate from us like a torch beam, but the light can equally be shone within the mind to illuminate thoughts. It is this ability to observe thoughts that the quote from Ajahn Chah addresses and the observer of thoughts and actions that he calls the knowing mind we will describe as a function of mind called *discriminating mind.* The thoughts and actions the beam illuminates might be recognised as simple conditioning – for example, hearing the bird's song and connecting the sound with the concept of the bird. If attention was concentrated, you won't even have been aware of the sound, but it might distract you from something you're doing. You then have a choice, either acknowledging the ideas evoked in your mind, surrendering them and returning to the task, or pursuing them and creating an imagined story. As we shall see, the choice is made by this function of discriminating mind, which can either observe clearly what arises or can become clouded and obscured by entanglement in the stories.

Just about every thought brings with it some sort of emotional tone, which may so subtle it is hardly noticed. However, emotions are not in themselves attachments. What transforms responding to the sound of the bird into attachment is not observing them from a detached perspective but becoming identified with them. Emotions are neither right nor wrong, but they can so easily draw us into attachment. This is how ego is formed, by forgetting what you are and becoming the story in your mind. Maintaining a watchful eye, they can be acknowledged, recognised as passing states and then allowed to subside without becoming identified and involved in them. This is how mind remains steady.

Describing the different functions of mind has a long history and earlier ideas have been superseded by increasing knowledge of how the brain works. In describing the functions of mind we will not be reviving outdated ideas, but we will also not be linking our system explicitly to brain physiology. The aim is to provide a way of understanding how the mind works from the perspective of Enlightened Living.

The first function of mind is *moving mind.* In part, this is the pathway that links our physical senses with the 'processor'. Moving mind comprises the sense impressions as well as their transmission – they can't meaningfully be separated. Moving mind is sometimes described as *discursive mind* and it also links thoughts together – one thought leading to another is moving mind. The connections made by mind when it is moving are constrained by the way it has been conditioned, but where it will end up is uncertain. Mind can career off in like an unguided missile, as we all know: we start by thinking about what we'll have for supper tonight and end up imagining triumphantly winning the argument we had yesterday which we actually lost! Mindfulness is about controlling the mind, not to prevent the associations that will inevitably arise from our conditioning but to prevent them from veering off unchecked into the realms of fantasy.

The way mind moves becomes very clear when we begin meditating. As the mind becomes still the movement of thoughts arising, being elaborated on and then passing as we move on to the next one becomes more apparent. It hasn't suddenly begun to move, it's just that the context – mind – in which the thoughts arise has become quieter and the movement more apparent. The wandering is constant, so a first step in controlling mind is to accept that it is an uncertain place. Mind is like Pandora's Box – she was warned not to open it!

However, the word 'control' has a very particular connotation of effortful and even frustrating endeavour. Anyone who has tried meditation knows how difficult it is to try to banish thoughts from the mind. What control means in mindful practice is recognising that moving mind will be drawn into imaginings, but rather than becoming entangled, just observing the thoughts as they arise and surrendering them by bringing attention back to the present. The thoughts then just come and go, without dragging you into them:

"When you sit in meditation, there may be various conditions of mind appearing, seeing and knowing all manner of things, experiencing different states. Don't keep track of them and don't get wrapped up in them. You only need to remind yourself that they're uncertain."

(Ajahn Chah: *Everything Arises, Everything Falls Away*)

A second function of mind, which we've already referred to, is *discriminating mind*. This is concerned with making choices about the information carried by moving mind. It might be a simple choice between one ice-cream flavour and another, but it is a subtle and very rapid process – even when we're excited and the words tumble out, we actually choose each word that we use, otherwise, we would just speak gibberish. Endless prattle may not have any purpose, but the words are nonetheless chosen. Discriminating mind chooses between things in the relative world, but what it is also able to know is the difference between what is true and what is not. What this means in Enlightened Living is knowing the difference between what is absolute and unchanging and what is a relative, passing state. In practical terms, it means knowing that what moving mind is throwing up are uncertain, passing states and the opportunity to not identify with them becomes available when discriminating mind is kept clear and still.

We've all seen this in our everyday experience, struggling to resolve a difficult problem which seems intractable. What can creep in is frustration or anger, which serves to further confuse the issue, but provided we can keep a 'clear head' – in other words, a still point from which to observe – the solution will often emerge. Discriminating mind free from the entanglement of ego is what provides this still point, from which there is a choice, either to identify with the passing state or to surrender it.

A third function of mind is c*onserving mind*, which is best understood as memory. Like moving mind, it has a physical aspect: what we're exposed to is established in the brain as part of the neural network. Memory activates the network and we remember. The conditioned, habitual ways we respond are stored in conserving mind and when we're faced with a task, the conserving and moving functions act in concert to recall the ways we've acted before. The decision about how to act is then determined by discriminating mind.

Although we're describing the different functions of mind independently they act in harmony, which is illustrated using straightforward examples like adding up the cost of groceries to see whether you have enough money available to purchase all of them. You check the prices and the registering and transmission of the price is carried out by moving mind. You remember how to add by drawing on knowledge held in conserving mind. The cumulative figures are brought together by moving mind and added using the arithmetic process held in memory. A decision about whether you can buy the articles or not is then made by discriminating mind, comparing the cost and the amount of available money.

With simple examples like this, it is relatively easy to identify the different functions of mind, but conserving mind is also the repository for all of the attachments we've formed. Using our example, you may have a preference for a particular brand of breakfast cereal but discover that the price has increased dramatically. Anger that it should have gone up by so much creeps in. You spot another brand which is cheaper and the despondency changes to triumph, but then you begin to doubt whether you'll like it as much as your usual one. You resign yourself to it, finish shopping but then find that despite the bargain you still don't have enough money. Elation changes to frustration, or embarrassment if you're already going through the check-out.

What has changed everything in the example is the addition of emotion. Emotion adds tone or quality to what is perceived or remembered: it adds feeling to knowing and depending on the tone it can turn the simple process of buying groceries into a nightmare. Emotion can be considered as a distinct function, *emotional mind.* We sometimes speak of making unemotional decisions, but emotion is almost always added to the mix, however subtle it might be. There is nothing wrong with emotion, but it is very much a double-edged sword: it may manifest as healing compassion or as destructive anger. Emotion can serve to dissolve the separation of ego, but can equally serve to facilitate attachment – it can form the glue that can bind us to things. The glue is ego and it isn't necessarily just emotions like anger. Ordinary 'love' is just as much an attachment and just as effective in clouding discriminating mind, as we shall see in Chapter 9.

Attachment is surrendered by *detachment*, though contrary to the way we might understand the word, detachment isn't an unemotional state. In fact, you can only avoid emotion by suppressing or diverting it in some way, which will lead to a closing of the heart. Emotion will arise and it facilitates selfless action as much as it facilitates attachments. Emotion is experienced by all sentient creatures, which provides a useful illustration. If you have a pet cat, watch it for a while. When it isn't sleeping there is mind and emotion at play, but functioning appropriately. For example, if a dog suddenly appears the cat experiences fear, which is immediately expressed as preparation for physical action: it hisses and its hair stands on end. Once the dog disappears, so too does the emotion – we know that because the cat's hair goes flat and it relaxes.

What your cat knows is that continuing to think afterwards about what the dog might or might not have done is pointless. The dog was there a while ago, but isn't any longer, so why continue to make the effort of thinking about it, provoking the whole physiological cascade of fight-or-flight when there's nothing to fight or flee from except a thought? Of course, we don't really know what cats think and we need to be cautious about using words like 'knowing' when describing cats and dogs, but if you bang the cat's bowl it will come running in search of food – it understands the connection, using discriminating mind. You might say that this is 'just conditioning', but that's also the case with most of the thinking and acting that humans engage in, habitual behaviours shaped by conditioning. We've already said that conditioning is a necessary and useful process, but the question is whether the habits are performed mindfully or not. Acting mindlessly from habit is no different from sleepwalking.

The real issue, though, is the attachments that may be formed from the conditioning. Going back to the cat's response, think back to the last time something happened to you that corresponds to the dog walking in, maybe the last time your boss gave a stinging criticism of some work you'd done. How often and for how long afterwards did you go on and on thinking about it? It would seem that most other animals behave almost entirely according to their conditioning. What sets us apart is the capacity to be self-aware and in this example to be aware of how this self wants revenge for having been criticised. Discriminating mind can be used intentionally to avoid all of that misery, by observing the emotion that arises but not identifying with it. When the discriminating mind is free of ego we can learn objectively from what the boss said – perhaps the work does need more attention to detail. The criticism might have been levelled inappropriately, in a state of anger, but that's the boss's problem, not yours. On the other hand, if everything in your workplace is said with anger discriminating mind would probably say the time has come to leave!

Ego involves thinking and can in some respects be seen as another function of mind, but the truth is that it doesn't really exist at all. Take our shopping example and the turmoil of embarrassment and shame that ensues if you discover at the checkout that you don't have the money to pay for the groceries. It is only ego that feels ashamed. The truth is that you don't have enough money and there's an end to it. Discriminating mind knows that any shame that might arise doesn't matter – it is just a passing emotional state. We imagine that we're learning from it and will never put ourselves in that position again, but learning doesn't happen by beating yourself up after the event. The consequence of the feeling of shame is separation: at that moment, you're separate from all of the happy shoppers who can pay. The sense of separation is ego. Knowing that it is a mistaken identity of what you are (consciousness) with what you are not (shame), it can be surrendered and it disappears. It never existed in the first place, other than as a mistaken idea fuelled by attachment.

The capacity to perceive ourselves as separate has probably developed along with brain: from an evolutionary perspective, there does seem to be a gradual emergence of a sense of oneself distinct from others and some other primates certainly seem to have a sense of self. What makes us unique is being able to choose to be free from the attachments that arise from ego and this is what liberation means. However, before we digress into more speculation about ourselves and other animals, from the perspective of Enlightened Living any similarities or differences between us and them are irrelevant, just as the similarities or differences between you and any other human being are irrelevant. All that matters is what you will do with the consciousness or attention that is undoubtedly available at this moment. It always is available.

Liberation is something you bring about, not by doing anything but by not doing anything; equally paradoxically, the sense of a separate 'you' disappears in the process. Using our way of looking at mind allows us to put some of the things that are said about it into perspective. It can be quite confusing to read some teachers speaking about killing or dispensing with mind. In deep meditation and deep sleep, it is true that mind does seem to disappear, but it is more that the functions we've described have become still. In these states, there isn't any thinking about things, but you continue to breathe, your heart beats. When the mind has completely ceased, they do too – it's called death – but even when your individual body and mind end, consciousness itself doesn't disappear. It will continue to be manifested in all of the forms; when life as we know it has ceased, consciousness manifesting as forms will remain.

What is really being described is not the killing of the mind but the killing of ego, a dissolving of the glue that has bound what we are to what we are not. When ego is surrendered conditioning remains, but free from being identified with what is observed. Liberation certainly means the end of ego, but not the end of mind. Sense impressions continue to register and to be offered to discriminating mind, using memory stored in conserving mind to determine our actions, but the need will only really be met if this process occurs without 'me' doing anything at all. Mind is then used to observe mind, which seems paradoxical until you distinguish between mind and ego.

Thinking based on ego is what ignorance is and in thinking, ego creates its own world. Shakespeare spells this out in the dialogue between Hamlet and Rosenkrantz about the state of Denmark:

Hamlet:
"Denmark's a prison."
Rosencrantz:
"Then is the world one."
Hamlet:
"A goodly one; in which there are many confines, wards, and dungeons, Denmark being one o' th' worst."
Rosencrantz:
"We think not so, my lord."
Hamlet:
"Why, then, 'tis none to you; for there is nothing either good or bad, but thinking makes it so. To me, it is a prison."

(Shakespeare: *Hamlet, Act 2 Scene II*)

In other words, thinking can lead to the attribution of value and meaning to things and these values and meanings are in the eye of the beholder.

There are many ways in which mind can be used, but the fundamental question is what it is devoted to. Devoting the life to ego is a life of selfishness, spent in ignorance; it is Shakespeare's tale told by an idiot, signifying nothing. Devoting the mind to meeting the need in the present, making consciousness available with no claim on it, is a fulfilled life, which means a life filled with untainted consciousness. Sounds simple and it is; what makes it so difficult is that for it to happen, the most treasured of all things – 'me' – has to be surrendered. To do this is to keep the mind under observation, to watch and to use discriminating mind without the formation of ego. What is then discovered is the still core of mind that is always available:

"Sense impressions come and trick (the untrained mind) into happiness, suffering, gladness and sorrow, but the mind's nature is none of those things... The untrained mind gets lost and follows these things; it forgets itself. Then we think that it is we who are upset or at ease or whatever. But really this mind is already unmoving and peaceful – really peaceful! Just like a leaf which remains still so long as the wind doesn't blow. If a wind comes up, the leaf flutters. The fluttering is due to the wind – the fluttering of the mind is due to those sense impressions; the mind follows them. If it doesn't follow them, it doesn't flutter. If we know fully the true nature of sense impressions, we will be unmoved."

(Ajahn Chah: *Food for the Heart*)

Our perceptions of things are formed as thoughts in our minds and we're drawn towards the things that give us pleasure and away from those that cause us pain. These desires and aversions become established in conserving mind as conditioned responses to things, but desires, aversions and their attendant conditioning are a natural process; the problem, as we've said, is attachment to the objects of that conditioning. Think about the last time you experienced the equivalent of some emergency event, the close call like the car veering in front of you in the example we used in Chapter 2. How many people have to hear about your near-death experience in the weeks and months afterwards? And is what you say happened what really happened? How much does it get elaborated or edited as the weeks go by? And most importantly, who is the central character around whom all of these stories revolve?

What actually happened was a sequence of causes and effects, the driver of the other car being distracted for a moment, that leading to the wheel being turned unintentionally, that leading to the car swerving, that leading to nearly colliding. Both drivers take evasive action and feel the emotion of relief if there isn't a collision, then drive on. That's all there was to it, cause and effect. We learn from the experience, but only in the moment. Reflecting on it afterwards may help to consolidate that learning, but it isn't done by just re-telling the story over and over. We keep going over things, imagining we're learning from them, but what happened even yesterday might just as well have happened a thousand years ago.

Mind can be a treacherous place, in which anything can be conjured up. To use it as an instrument it needs to be kept under observation: we need to be aware as much as possible of what's arising in mind and what these thoughts might trigger. Treat it like an extremely sharp knife: used without conscious attention and it will injure you. Knowing happiness, unhappiness or any other variety of emotion means to observe it arise and pass, without becoming entangled in it. The misery that follows from churning over emotional upset is a self-inflicted injury. This is why the only thing to be done in this teaching is to observe. Not to try to change anything, just to observe and since all actions originate in mind, it is mind that needs to be observed. Change may or may not occur, according to the measure of things we will describe in Chapter 7, but seeking to change things is a diversion. The relative world is just change: forms constantly being transformed through the process of cause and effect, constantly becoming something different. To be concerned with change is to be locked into time, setting goals for the future and wanting something different from the past. Detached observing can only happen in the present. Experiences and anticipations will arise, but rather than becoming identified with them they can be observed and seen for what they so often are: distorted perceptions of what has happened and hopes for what we want to happen.

Detached observation depends on discriminating mind not being clouded by ego and is the 'knowing' in the earlier quote from Ajahn Chah:

"What's it like to encounter moods and emotions? What's it like to be without any defiled emotions whatsoever? That which knows these things is what is meant by the 'knowing'."

(Ajahn Chah: *Food for the Heart*)

It is discriminating mind that knows and what it knows is that the thoughts and emotions are uncertain and passing. So what is a 'defiled emotion'? Emotions are just emotions and they will arise. Defilement is attachment and when that occurs, emotion becomes the agent that binds us. A practical way to discover this is to watch what you say. Speech doesn't just happen, it starts as a thought in the mind, so observing the action of speech is, in fact, observing the action of mind. When Jesus was challenged by the scribes and Pharisees because his disciples had eaten without first washing their hands, he said:

"*There is nothing from without a man that entering into him can defile him: but the things which come out of him, those are they that defile a man.*

If any man has ears to hear, let him hear.

And when he was entered into the house from the people, his disciples asked him concerning the parable.

And he said, that which cometh out of the man, that defileth the man.

For from within, out of the heart of men, proceed evil thoughts, adulteries, fornications, murders.

Thefts, covetousness, wickedness, deceit, lasciviousness, an evil eye, blasphemy, pride, foolishness.

All these evil things come from within and defile the man."

(*Mark 7:15–21*)

The context leads Jesus to describe speech as defiling us, but speech can equally reflect the truth. The question is, what determines this choice? In other words, to what are our words dedicated? For speech to reflect the truth, ego needs to be dissolved so that discriminating mind can be used appropriately. This is discovered in practice, by listening to what we say. This can seem impossible, but try it yourself. It is important that it doesn't become contrived, but observing what we say provides a clear illustration of how the mind can indeed watch the mind.

Of all the practices we can bring into our daily lives, hearing what we ourselves say provides direct access to the mind, where all of the words and stories are formed. When they're under the influence of ego they can be seen as an endless 'doing'. This is not just imagining oneself doing any particular thing – more subtle than that is the 'me' to whom all of these thoughts are dedicated. This separate individual can be deeply embedded and so implicit in our view of the world that everything is perceived from the perspective of ego.

"All claims of being the doer of actions or enjoyer of objects relates to ego. When wisdom dawns, then the distinction between the witness and the doer becomes clear and one understands that one is the witness and not the doer or enjoyer. The witness is the stillness; the claims of doing and enjoying are the din of the market, the realm of movement... As long as there is the feeling of doing and achieving, the individual is in the movement and not in stillness."

(Shantanand Saraswati: *Good Company*)

Observing ego in action requires acute observation and to see it clearly we need to observe with detached indifference. Indifference generally has very negative connotations, but as we've already explained, what it means here is that there is no difference: happiness and unhappiness are just values and meanings we've attached to a passing state of the mind. When we do observe with indifference we usually discover thoughts arising continuously and also that we can end up becoming involved in relationships with those thoughts. We become the actor in endless imagined dramas, attached to and identified with, stories concocted by ego. All to no avail.

We might be hurrying to a meeting and find ourselves at the back of a queue of traffic. Ego tells us that the traffic was put there to prevent us getting to the meeting and we end up impatient and angry. We even have the ignorant phrases to console ourselves with: 'I was justifiably angry'. Anger may well arise in the mind but it can just as quickly be seen and surrendered. Anger is never justified and serves no purpose. You eventually get to the meeting and go on and on about how angry you were, inviting everyone else to collaborate in it with you, but for all your anger, what happened to the traffic queue? It didn't move an inch. As Jesus said, no one can add a cubit to his stature by taking thought. A more useful question is to ask why you're always so angry! Observe the mind to discover why.

The practice is not to somehow stop these thoughts – they will arise. The practice is to not identify with them. All of this identifying with thoughts or not identifying with thoughts takes place in mind and mind is used to observe the process. In other words, mind is being used to observe mind, and when attachments formed within it are surrendered, mind remains. You can't become mindless, any more than you can become emotionless. The purpose of surrendering attachments is so that mind can operate naturally, discriminating between things and acting according to what is needed.

Chapter 4
Attachment and Liberation

Enlightenment follows from the surrender of attachments, so what exactly are these attachments? It is helpful to put this question into the context of ego since ego can actually be defined as the sum of our attachments. The way we described it in Chapter 1 was to refer to the Vedic tradition, where the equivalent Sanskrit word for ego is *ahankara*. As we saw, the word is a compound of two words, aham and kara; the rules of Sanskrit grammar turn the 'm' into an 'n' when the two words are combined. Aham translates loosely as 'I am', while kara refers to any form, whether it be a person, a tree or a thought. We illustrated ego in Chapter 1 by using a simple 'I am…' sentence completion exercise, for example:

I am a man/woman
I am sad/happy
I am beautiful/ugly

For each statement, the part on the left – 'I am' – remains the same. Everything on the right-hand side is different and is also constantly changing: I might be sad one minute, happy the next. It is an analogy, but it illustrates ego precisely. The left-hand side of the statement represents *being* (aham), and the right-hand side the relative world of *becoming* (kara).

Everything in the relative world is becoming something else: an infant becomes a child, a child becomes an adolescent, an adolescent becomes an adult, an adult ages and becomes a corpse. 'I am', consciousness with nothing added, is changeless. We've said that consciousness is known only by its reflection through our minds and bodies as attention; is the attention you give as an adult any different from the attention you gave as a child? Experience has been added, conditioning and attachments have increased, but attention is the same. Aham stands for the consciousness of which everything (kara) is a form. In truth, you are not a man or a woman or sad or happy – these are just passing forms, changing in accordance with the law of cause and effect. The mistake is thinking that you *are* the form and ignoring the source of the form, consciousness.

The world is filled with innumerable forms. At a molecular level, all forms are made up the same elements but in the world of our direct experience, each form is separate and different from every other one. There may be family similarities: all tigers are forms of large cat and have stripes, but no two tigers are exactly identical. This is the relative realm, where the separate forms cannot be made into one. Following the convention we referred to in Chapter 1, in this realm what we call 'me' is described as *self*; the forms are all forms of a single consciousness, described as *Self*. What we are in essence, then, is consciousness, 'I am' with nothing added. When aham becomes identified with something in the world, consciousness becomes attached to that form, instead of being acknowledged as a form that consciousness has taken on temporarily:

"If one hangs a coat in the wardrobe, the inanimate coat can't put itself on anyone's body. It will remain where it is. When you put it on, it goes with you everywhere. So it is with the body. The body is the coat; if you claim the body as your own, then it accompanies you everywhere, but as soon as you stop claiming, then it takes its proper place as part of nature. Then the 'I' becomes the witness, having no attachment."

(Shantanand Saraswati: *Good Company*)

This is the mistake of ego: there is in truth only one consciousness giving rise to myriad forms, but once attachments occur there is identification with the form. The separation that follows from attachment leads to feelings of isolation and a desire to belong. The paradox of the human condition is wanting to be unique and separate, but at the same time desperately wanting to be part of something together with others we see as the same as us, be it a club, a religion or a nation. Our similarity to these others is signalled by our attitudes, our beliefs or the colour of our skin, which in turn makes 'us' separate from 'them' and we don't need to look far to see the consequences. The real paradox is that the similarities we seek are illusory and simply a consequence of conditioning: by chance alone, our parents may have held similar beliefs, or we possess the genes that make our skin white or black. The sense of belonging is a sentimental attachment to these conditioned differences and sentimentality is not necessarily as benign as it sounds – it is also the source of racism and war.

When ego arises through the mistaken identification of what I am with what I am not, what is created is a perception of being a separate entity. What I am separate from is all of the other entities, though most importantly, from other people who are not like me – separateness is the very quality of ego and clubs, nations and religions form a kind of group ego. Identifying with something that makes us separate from others is the source of all of the misery in the world. How could you inflict torture or pain on anything that is known to be a form of the same consciousness as yourself? Because the forms are separate, it is a short step to seeing the other as a rival. This is the scarcity principle, that everything is in limited supply and I need to get as much of it for myself as I can. What's available in the relative world is limited. Once gone it will not be replenished: extinction is irreversible. Some resources are self-renewing, but only if they are managed in a measured way. Governed by the greed of ego, humans seem bent on using it all up as quickly as possible, without regard for the principle of measure which is described in Chapter 7.

Ajahn Chah once said that he didn't know any rich people, only people who wanted more. From this greed arise jealousy, anger, even love in its relative and temporary form. When we 'love' someone we feel that there is a special bond and we want desperately to become one with that person. Impossible, since the forms of body and mind are separate and will remain so, but if the attachments to body and mind are surrendered, what can then be discovered is that you are one, not just with that person but with all forms. This is why when people try to describe the experience of liberation, they will often use words like 'unity' or 'oneness'. The problem for ego is that you will no longer have this unity for yourself since unity can only arise when you've removed yourself! Seen clearly, wanting something for me will always lead to misery. We are all to varying degrees egotistical, judging the world from the perspective of ego and we get frustrated and angry with people because they're not doing what ego wants or expects them to.

This highlights another paradox of Enlightened Living: there's nothing in it for anybody, in other words, there's no benefit in enlightenment for any separate individual. To live in an enlightened way isn't personal. We're unfortunately conditioned to seeking effects and benefits, but they're part of the relative world and have no intrinsic value or meaning. Which is not to say we should avoid acting to relieve suffering. The world of forms is a relative one where wealth and poverty, sickness and health are all unevenly distributed and always will be. By contrast, consciousness is unlimited and always available, irrespective of our particular relative circumstance. We may lack material wealth, but the things that make up the material world have no intrinsic value: when we envy someone materially richer than ourselves we're envying something valueless.

Ego is a thought-form and doesn't actually exist other than as a perception of separateness. Here are some examples of what teachers from different traditions have said about ego:

"You are not those thoughts which are turning, turning in your mind; you are not those changing feelings; you are not the different decisions you make and the different wills you have; you are not that separate ego."

(Shantanand Saraswati: *Good Company*)

"When suffering arises, we attach to the suffering and thereby must really suffer. In the same way, when happiness arises, we attach to the happiness and consequently experience pleasure. Attachment to these feelings gives rise to the concept of self or ego and thoughts of 'we and 'they' continually manifest. Here is where it all begins and then it carries us around in its never-ending cycle."

(Ajahn Chah: *Food for the Heart*)

Q: What is the ego-self? How is it related to the real Self?
A: "*The ego-self appears and disappears and is transitory, whereas the real Self is permanent. Though you are actually the true Self, you wrongly identify the real Self with the ego-self.*"
Q: One must sublimate the ego-self into the true Self.
A: "*The ego-self does not exist at all.*"
Q: Why does it give us trouble?
A: "*To whom is the trouble? The trouble also is imagined. Trouble and pleasure are only for the ego.*"

(Godman (Ed): *Be as You Are – The Teachings of Ramana Maharshi*)

Although ego doesn't actually exist except as a mistaken belief, the belief that we are separate binds us tightly. The paradox is that we are never bound, we only think we are because of the mistaken bondage of ego. In the book *Good Company*, Shantanand Saraswati tells the story of the washer man who asked his son to take a load of washing to the river on his donkeys. The donkeys wouldn't budge, until the washer man told his son that when he returned home with them in the evening he touched their hooves as if he was binding them, then in the morning touched them again, pretending to loosen the bonds. His son does the same and the donkeys move. The moral of the story is that the donkeys didn't move because they thought they were bound; just so with ego, we think we're bound, when in truth we're not.

Attention left to its own devices conjures up the thoughts turning, turning in the mind. These may be simple associations formed by conditioning, but ego crystallises out of them when we become attached. The reason for identifying with something is mostly impression management: conveying to the world at large an image of me that fits with what ego desires. This might range from wanting to be a hero to being a victim, being all-conquering or all-suffering – it encompasses the full range. The effect of becoming identified with something is separation, confirming that I belong to a category of forms that is separate from other forms. Even thinking of myself as someone who likes peanut butter can lead to seeing myself as separate from those who do not.

Test it for yourself: notice what arises in the mind when someone says that they don't like something you do like, be it dogs, cats, walking, cycling, or peanut butter. Then notice what arises when someone says they really love something that you love too. You dislike the first person because they're different from you and like the second because they like what you like. All this liking and disliking starts as conditioning, such as trying peanut butter and either liking it or not, but through attachment, it becomes difference and separateness and when there's more than peanut butter at stake, it becomes war and killing.

To avoid attachment, the fundamental step is acknowledging that 'I am' is the undivided consciousness that is the source of all forms. When this knowledge docs arise, the world doesn't change. Liberation is ordinary; what is extraordinary is the determination to stay separate, even though it means a life of bondage and misery! The solution is not to identify with others who appear to be similar to ourselves – those similarities are illusory and lead inevitably to further separation between 'our group' and those who belong to a different one. The way out is to surrender the attachments, to allow things to occur as they will but to make sure you remain untouched by them. Ajahn Chah expressed it as follows:

"If your house is flooded or burnt to the ground, allow that threat to affect only your house. If there's a flood, don't let it flood your mind. If there's a fire, don't let it burn your heart. Let it be merely the house – which is outside – that is flooded or burned. Now is the time to allow the mind to let go of attachments."

(Ajahn Chah: *Food for the Heart*)

The solution is also not determinedly avoiding being with people who do think in a similar way to you. We are attracted to like-minded people, but you can keep their company without seeing yourself and them as separate from others with different ways of thinking. What Ajahn Chah is describing is indifference, the same indifference that is illustrated in the story of the Zen master Hakuin. In the story, Hakuin is accused of fathering a child. The girl's parents are outraged and insist that he take the child and raise it, which he does; his only comment is, 'Is that so?' The girl later admits that the father was actually a young man who worked in the fish market.

"The mother and father of the girl at once went to Hakuin to ask his forgiveness, to apologise at length and to get the child back again. Hakuin was willing. In yielding the child, all he said was, 'Is that so?'"

(Paul Reps: *Zen Flesh, Zen Bones*)

For the most part, what forges the attachment to something is emotion. Emotion is just emotion – passing happiness or misery – but unless it is watched, it will become the glue of ahankara, binding what you are to what you are not. 'Watching the mind' is mindfulness and in that state, emotion isn't transformed into glue. After all, there have to be two things to join for the glue to have any effect. It follows that attachment can't occur when there is unity, so attachment ends when separation ends, but this can seem a daunting prospect: liberation often seems so fleeting. The mistake is to see it as fleeting and to regret that it seems so short-lived. What that does is to place liberation firmly back in the relative world of time. It doesn't matter how fleeting it may be. When liberation occurs we are for that moment free from becoming. Liberation is a synonym for enlightenment. What we're liberated from is the false belief that I am the form or forms I've become attached to, but it isn't 'me' that is liberated; in fact, it is 'me' that consciousness is liberated from! Enlightenment means there's nobody there to claim anything. As we've said, there's nothing for me to gain from enlightenment.

Liberation can only be in the moment – liberation yesterday or tomorrow is just a thought about liberation – and it doesn't particularly matter if attachment reinstates itself in the next moment. Although it may come and go, the moment of liberation is all or none: you can't be partly liberated, although in our experience the movement from being bound to being free does appear to be progressive. For example, compare the degree of attachment before and after beginning to practice mindfulness. Initially, remembering tends to be a haphazard affair, but as ignorance is dispelled it becomes more and more steadfast:

"We determine to make our minds resolute, but it's hard. We resolve to do a certain practice; we say we'll practice in this way – but only a day or two goes by, maybe just a few hours and we forget all about it. We then remember and try to make our minds firm again. 'This time I'll do it right!' Shortly afterward, we are pulled away by one of our senses and it falls apart again. So we start all over again! This is how it is. Like a poorly built dam, our practice is weak. And it goes on like this until we arrive at true wisdom. Once we penetrate to the truth, we are freed from everything. Only peace remains."

(Ajahn Chah: *Food for the Heart*)

In other words, what is progressive and incremental is not enlightenment itself but the practice of mindfulness towards enlightenment. Which is not to say that liberation is once and for all. There are no 'fully realised beings', for whom no further need for practice is necessary – constant vigilance is always required. The problem is with the intention of the practice. As long as liberation remains something we're determined to achieve it will remain elusive and we'll feel disappointed each time attachment reasserts itself. The final surrender is the very desire to be enlightened. There's a story that illustrates it: a king places his throne at the end of the garden and proclaims that anyone who walks through the garden and sits on it can have the kingdom. Along the path to the throne, the king arranges temptations: beautiful men and women, money, all the things that draw us into greed and addiction and the final temptation is the claim on enlightenment itself. All who attempt the pathway fail, until the simple gardener (the wise are always simple gardeners or servants in these stories) walks through untouched by temptation and claims the kingdom of unattached liberation.

The enduring discipline of practice is essential. Rather like meditation, there does need to be the steadfast adherence to the practice for it to happen at all, but discipline isn't suffering. Again, surrender is needed: you remember that you 'should' meditate now, but there's that report you'd like to finish. If you do sit down to meditate your mind will be filled with the report; if you do the report, you feel guilty about not meditating! This is just a struggle. What's required is an indifferent evaluation of the need: maybe the report is in fact more pressing, in which case do the report, without any guilt. To make a decision like this requires a clear discriminating mind and discipline then becomes moving freely rather than turmoil and suffering.

What removes attachment is love, but only the love we will describe in Chapter 9. Love is generally predicated on separation, loving one person but hating another, or even loving and then hating the same person. This is sentimentality. What love is, is the acknowledgement of no difference between one form and another – you and your neighbour, for example, or you and a tree or a rock. You don't need to become a tree hugger; in fact, you don't need to 'do' anything at all, just acknowledge the unity of absolute consciousness. This isn't something momentous, to be done with an assumed reverence or hushed 'spirituality'. Liberation is ordinary and the world goes on as it always will, a mechanical process of cause and effect. The difference is living in it and enjoying, but without claiming any of it at all:

> *"Everything that lives is full of the Lord;*
> *Enjoy – do not covet His property."*
>
> (*Isha Upanishad*)

The perceived difference between forms is a consequence of conditioning. A tiger doesn't suddenly become a deer, because its form has been conditioned by biological processes like DNA. Each tiger is in turn different from every other one, again as a result of the particular individual conditioning that has occurred. Rocks are a conditioned form of elements like iron, or compressed sediments. Likewise, the behaviour you might like or not like in someone has been conditioned into the form. Being able to see this is a useful step away from separation, acknowledging that how that person looks or what they like or don't like can be understood from their conditioning. For example, you talk to someone who seems completely uninterested in what you're saying and you see your irritation rising. What gets irritated is ego. Ego attaches great significance and value to itself; how can anyone not be interested in what it has to say?

You then remember to take a perspective other than that dictated by ego and ask whether there's a problem. It turns out that this person's relationship has recently ended, or someone close to them has recently died. From a purely philosophical perspective, all that has happened when someone dies is that the form of body and mind has ceased, as they all must. To say as much to this person would certainly not be meeting the need, it would more likely be an attachment to you showing what a detached philosopher you are. Showing genuine compassion for the person isn't ignorance. Even with a lot of practice, we may still succumb to feelings of loss and despair, that's just how it is. Enlightened Living isn't a prescription.

All that we can observe is the conditioning and the attachment to the fruit of the conditioning and it is the attachment that needs to be surrendered. Attachments are undermined not by feeling nothing at all, but by ensuring that there is no attachment to the feeling:

"The natural state of the mind is neither happiness nor unhappiness. When feeling enters the mind, happiness or unhappiness is born. If we are mindful, we know pleasant feeling as pleasant feeling. The mind that knows will not pick it up. Happiness is there but it's 'outside' the mind, not buried within it. The mind simply knows the feeling clearly."

(Ajahn Chah: *Food for the Heart*)

Not only do we tend to see liberation as something to be achieved, we also place it into the context of opposites – there is attachment and there is liberation; attachment is bad and liberation is good. If you rely on opposites like this, then liberation is defined by attachment or the absence of it. We think we need to search to find liberation, when in truth, just like the washer man's donkeys, we are never bound. If we think there's bondage we're then bound to seek freedom from it, but what if there never was any bondage in the first place? Here's what Ramana Maharshi said in answer to a question about *mukti* or liberation:

"The word mukti is so provoking. Why should one seek it? One believes there is bondage and therefore seeks liberation. But the fact is that there is no bondage but only liberation. Why call it a name and seek it?"

(Godman (Ed): *Be as You Are – The Teachings of Ramana Maharshi*)

The idea that there is a journey to be undertaken and a treasure to be found is just a misleading myth. If you think liberation is elusive and requires a long struggle you'll have a long struggle and find nothing. Trying to 'do' liberation is like doing anything: there is a doer and something to be done, to be achieved, yet another fulfilment of desire. We make the same false distinction between being the doer and not being the doer of actions when in truth there isn't a doer at all. What believes it does things and achieves things is merely ego. Things do get done by the integrated actions of body and mind to meet a perceived need, but consciousness does nothing. How could it, if it is both doer and what's done, both observer and observed? What does things is body and mind and since you can observe them, you can't be them.

The difficulty with this view is that if it is true, then why would we bother to do anything at all? Leave out the 'bother', just surrender being the doer by responding to the need. Actions won't stop, but they'll be performed by body and mind acting in concert, watched by consciousness and without attachment to the fruit of the action. The issue is with the idea of doing, all of it dedicated to achieving something. Instead, as we'll see in Chapter 8, all that's required is surrender, just letting go. Being a 'doer' is a recipe for resentment: 'why do I always have to do everything round here?'

There's a story about how to catch monkeys. You take a pot with a hole in it just big enough for the monkey to squeeze its hand in. Tie the pot to the ground, put one peanut inside and hide behind a tree. The monkey runs up, inserts its hand and grabs the peanut, but now it has a fist that's too big to pull back out through the hole. The pot's tied to the ground, so you just run up and catch the monkey – it won't let go of the peanut. The paradox is that the forest is full of food and the monkey gives up its life for a peanut. To be free from the attachment to that peanut, all it had to do was open its fist and let go. Why do we think liberation is an effort that's going to take a lifetime? Liberation is available anytime, all the time; just let go.

Of course, attachments are strong and no sooner have you surrendered one than it reinstates itself or is replaced by another. Well, that's how it is. Conditioning won't stop and desire and aversion will continue to try to creep in and forge attachments. Just keep on letting go, moment to moment. The idea is to be able to surrender the principle of holding on, rather than a progressive letting go of each attachment in turn until there are none left – there are so many already formed or still being formed, including the desire to get to the end of them all, that it will never happen that way. Although liberation is in truth all-or-none, in practice it requires constant vigilance, watching with growing mindfulness for the trap of attachment. This is not vigilance as in some sort of sleepless effort, but watching the mind as constantly as you're able to. Right now, stop reading for a moment, close your eyes and observe the thoughts in your mind. It doesn't require any effort; the only effort starts when you become identified with them and concoct stories, or try to banish them from your mind. The practice that leads to enlightenment and liberation is observing and then surrendering attachments.

In Chapter 2 we described an exercise in mindfulness, just listening with your eyes closed. You can extend the exercise by again closing your eyes and becoming aware of your body on the chair. If there is any tension held in your body, let that go and relax. That's relatively easy and it gives the opportunity to allow any tension in your body to dissolve. You can deepen that relaxation by being aware of your breathing, the cool sensation as you breathe in, and the warm sensation as you breathe out. With each out-breath, allow any residual tension to dissolve. Then move your attention to being aware of the thoughts in your mind. Don't try to stop them, but resist taking them up and entertaining them. Just notice how they arise and pass, how they move in and out of awareness. Continue for as long as you feel comfortable, then open your eyes again.

When we try an exercise like this, we often find our minds initially shifting almost uncontrollably from observing thoughts to becoming identified with them, but gradually we are more and more able to just watch them arise and pass from a point which remains steady and doesn't become involved. Observing body and mind like this, we can know that we are observing from a still point. Mind will move – as we saw in Chapter 3, that's one of its functions. Moving mind is designed to do just that, but you have a choice, either to become involved in the movement or to observe it happening. Body and mind then become instruments that we can use to meet the need. Like any tool, they can be used in ignorant or truthful ways, which will depend on the clarity of discriminating mind. When we open our eyes after the exercise the conditioned relative world rushes back in. You will probably have noticed the way it does so and with mindfulness, you may also have seen that the 'doing' that follows has an intention: to control. There are phrases we might use to counter this, such as 'Not my will, but Thy will be done', but it will remain a mere concept as long as 'Thy' remains a separate entity rather than your own Self.

This is where faith enters into our practice. Faith is ordinarily thought of as surrendering to a greater power – 'Thy will' is the will of God. In doing so, there is me and God and we end up convincing ourselves we're doing what an instrumental Creator would like or prefer us to do. This is faith in the ordinary sense, a belief in what cannot be known directly with the mind and which remains yet another concept. A different and more challenging way is to have faith in uncertainty. Nothing in the universe is certain. We live in the world; to live in it but not of it is to relinquish control by acknowledging that it is at all times uncertain. This doesn't mean thinking that everything you're familiar with will suddenly disappear, or anxiously trying to anticipate good or bad things that might happen. What is now is substantially now, but whether it will exist in a second, minute, or hour is uncertain. This is an incontrovertible fact, but so much of what we do and think is a vain attempt to contradict uncertainty by controlling everything.

Surrendering control should not be mistaken for fatalism. There is no room in Enlightened Living for phrases like, 'you get what you were meant to get', or 'it was meant to be'. Meant by whom? There isn't a controlling deity, just the law of cause and effect. Sometimes, it happens in a very obvious way – throw something in the air and it will come down again. The links between the causes and the effects may be a lot more complex, but simple or complex, they're actually not relevant. Causes and effects are locked in time; enlightenment is now. Once there is an acknowledgement that everything is uncertain, it becomes much easier to rest in the now and relinquish the desire to control. When we become frustrated we usually look for something or someone to blame, which transforms frustration into anger. What control actually means is having things my way and all this drama arises because the world isn't the way I want it to be.

Relinquishing control doesn't preclude planning, or drawing on the experience of what happened the last time you did something. If the result last time didn't meet the need, you will want to respond differently this time, but 'this time' is now. You can only actually act in the present. What we do when we maintain a detached frame of mind will be informed by memories, held in the conserving mind we described in Chapter 3, but monitored by an uncontaminated discriminating mind.

Surrendering to the moment is unconditional. There's a well-known story that illustrates it: A man slips off a cliff, but manages to grab a branch half-way down. He can't climb back up and below him is a thousand-foot drop. He calls upon God to help him and swears that if God saves him he will from then on be absolutely devout. God has heard all this before and tells the man so. The man pleads with God, saying his faith is now absolute and unswerving. "In that case," says God, "let go the branch."

One way of interpreting the story is that if the man really has faith, he will trust completely, let go and God will save him. But what if he lets go and falls to his death? Has God failed to keep his end of the bargain? In real faith, there are no deals; this isn't a marketplace and there are no bargains, just what is. Connecting with the present doesn't require faith – you don't need to believe in what you can observe. What is needed, paradoxically, is faith in uncertainty. Here's another cliff-hanger: a man is chased by a tiger and climbs down a cliff to escape. Half-way down he realises there's another tiger waiting at the bottom. He then spies a succulent wild strawberry growing just next to his hand; he picks the strawberry and enjoys its luscious taste. The message is that whatever might befall him in the next minute or so is uncertain; the strawberry is now.

Having faith in uncertainty means a faith that is unwavering. The reason why faith wavers is because we end up expecting something in return, like expecting that if the man on the cliff lets go he will be saved. Faith is unwavering when whatever the outcome, there is acceptance of it. This applies to our approach to Enlightened Living. It will often begin with an acknowledgement that what has been pursued in the life has not led to satisfaction and a search begins for a different way of living. In tandem with devotion to the practice, resistance to it may also grow, mainly because of the expectation of something in return. We've already said there's nothing in enlightenment for anybody – it is about surrendering, not gaining.

There can come a point where being drawn to pursuing truth is finely balanced against giving up. What then? Do we continue to nurture ideas about where it might lead? Practising this teaching to the full means that whatever presents itself is weighed by discriminating mind and if it accords with the truth then that is what is followed. What happens next is neither good nor bad but uncertain:

"It all comes down to this. Things that are uncertain will not become otherwise. If you see something to be exceedingly good, some problems will come about for you. If you see something as extremely bad, will that help you? If you follow these two ways, you are experiencing the two extremes the Buddha warned about. You have indulgence and self-torment within you. But if you put them both down, good and evil, where will you dwell? When you are not following the ways of good or bad, what is there? It's nothing that can be fixated on and objectively known."

(Ajahn Chah: *Being Dharma*)

This helps us make sense of what Jesus said:

"*And it came to pass, that, as they went in the way, a certain man said unto him, Lord, I will follow thee whithersoever thou goest.*

And Jesus said unto him, Foxes have holes and birds of the air have nests, but the Son of man hath not where to lay his head."

(*Luke 9:57–58*)

Enlightenment means being nobody, which ego definitely isn't interested in. Not having anywhere to lay your head is not a cry of despondency, it is a metaphor for not being attached, for being the 'passer-by' that Jesus refers to in the Gospel of Thomas. What Jesus says to the next man is startling:

"*And he said unto another, Follow me. But he said, Lord, suffer me first to go and bury my father.*

Jesus said unto him, Let the dead bury the dead: but go thou and preach the kingdom of God."

(*Luke 9:59–60*)

Living a life governed by ego is death in life. A funeral attended by forms dominated by ego is the dead burying the dead. To want to become a disciple in the first place, this man must have seen the attachments; Jesus was encouraging him to take the final step to liberation by surrendering them, though from the perspective of Enlightened Living we might want to rephrase the last part as 'go thou, surrender attachments and live in the now'!

Chapter 5
Emptiness and Fulfilment

The title of the previous chapter is couched in opposites: attachment and liberation. As we shall see in this chapter, emptiness and fulfilment are paradoxically one and the same. Fulfilment comes from emptiness, but this isn't the emptiness of nothing there. Enlightenment doesn't require giving away all that you own, but it does mean surrendering the attachment to the things we consider ours.

Mindfulness is an ancient Buddhist practice which is central to enlightenment. One of the problems with the way the word is currently used is giving it a purpose: improving our lives, or making us happier. Improvement and happiness are what ego strives for; enlightenment is about dispensing with ego. In the same way, we often speak of seeking fulfilment in our lives, but the question is, what's being filled and with what? Mostly, fulfilment is the happiness that comes from achieving some goal or other – completing a degree, for example, or being promoted to a more senior role at work, or even something more everyday like having a fine meal. Don't we find that after a relatively short period of time we're wondering 'what's next?' This is most obvious with food. Even if you overeat – literally fill yourself full – it won't be long before you're hungry again.

With bodily needs like food, water or air the need is a genuine one since without them we would die, but much of what we're fulfilling in our daily lives are wants rather than needs. Wants are desires for things on which life doesn't depend, like more money, more status, more everything. In fact, this is even true for a need like food – how common is it that we eat just enough to satisfy hunger? We're driven to continue eating or to force ourselves to stop eating, by conditioning that has become attachment. The body is conditioned to know when it has had the sufficient amount, but attachment drives us to eat more, or to starve ourselves.

So how much is 'sufficient'? We'll be exploring that in more detail in Chapter 7, which is about measure and choice, but the way to find out about how attached we are is to keep watching. You can only observe what's happening now, so this requires being in the present – eating with presence of mind, for example, consciously being aware of when we've had sufficient and stopping; thereby, surrendering the attachment. It is ego that continues to demand indulgence beyond measure. Ego can creep in very subtly, so we need to keep watching if we're to avoid claiming the very act of surrender, making sure everyone knows how disciplined we are by stopping; perhaps most of all, becoming a passer-by means surrendering the desire to be famous.

Eating in a more conscious way doesn't mean adopting a reverential seriousness about the process. That's just posturing and although we do have to eat to live, just consuming food to ensure we get enough protein, energy and the like is utilitarian. Preparing food, combining ingredients in various ways, all of this is intended to make the food tastier and hence more enjoyable. Once enlightenment becomes serious we've forgotten what the Isha Upanishad tells us in the quote we used in Chapter 4:

> *"Everything that lives is full of the Lord;*
> *Enjoy – do not covet His property."*
>
> (*Isha Upanishad*)

In other words, everything is filled with consciousness and is there to enjoy. Describing forms as vessels of consciousness can be misleading, since the forms themselves are forms of consciousness, as is the space between the forms. Using concepts in a metaphorical way can be helpful provided we remember they are just metaphors used to aid understanding, and we can resist the temptation to digress into intellectual gymnastics by simply acknowledging that we do feel enjoyment. What distorts that simple enjoyment, however, is what the Upanishad describes as coveting the fruit of the enjoyment, becoming so attached to the pleasure that we're unable to stop. This is greed, wanting it for me and wanting more and more. It helps to think of what becoming a passer-by actually means: you pass by things, so the opportunity to enjoy them is only available while they're there; once passed, there's no longing or regret and no attempt to make them last longer than their measure.

Restrictive dieting might not seem like greed but it is, claiming the fruit of self-denial and setting up yet another ego trap: you decide to cut out chocolate altogether and every time you see or smell chocolate you have to force yourself to not have any. You then feel you can reward yourself by indulging a bit and you polish off a whole box. This leads to guilt and then deprivation again, in a cycle of struggle. Have chocolate, but just enough. What knows how much is enough is discriminating mind, but only when it is operating freely, uncontaminated by attachments. Greed limits our choices to the extremes of denial or indulgence; practising measure offers a third point from which discriminating mind can determine appropriate actions.

With physical needs like food and water, we can relatively easily see the growing thirst or hunger for what it is, a bodily need for energy or water, but much of what drives ego is a more insidious and complex process that can be difficult to keep under observation. Take work as an example: it requires a refinement of discriminating mind to see that it isn't so much being promoted that's important but the enjoyment of the job itself. Of course, we feel good when we've worked diligently and have been rewarded for it, but promotion is a by-product. We often talk about job-satisfaction, but what do we mean by that? We're often caught both ways: we work hard and get the reward we expect and ego fills with pride; we work hard but someone else gets the credit and ego fills with resentment. The problem is that word 'expect'. We're constantly striving, being driven to achieve something or another, only to feel a growing dissatisfaction again once it has been achieved or disappointment if it hasn't. We may even end up wishing we hadn't been promoted – it isn't uncommon for someone to be promoted to being a manager when they'd far prefer to be doing the hands-on work. Disliking the management role then becomes yet another attachment, an aversion rather than a desire, but an attachment nonetheless.

This is being attached to the fruit of the action, regretting decisions made or racing off into the future to secure the next goal. What is missed altogether is the present. What are you racing towards? All sentient forms have the same end, they die, so this is a life spent racing towards your death, never satisfied by anything. Shakespeare described the ordinary life of striving perfectly:

> "To-morrow and to-morrow and to-morrow,
> Creeps in this petty pace from day to day,
> To the last syllable of recorded time;
> And all our yesterdays have lighted fools
> The way to dusty death. Out, out, brief candle!
> Life's but a walking shadow, a poor player
> That struts and frets his hour upon the stage,
> And then is heard no more; it is a tale
> Told by an idiot, full of sound and fury,
> Signifying nothing."
>
> (William Shakespeare: *Macbeth, Act 5 scene V*)

This might seem a cynical view and in one sense it is, we would hardly hold Macbeth up as a paragon of enlightened practice. Judging from the play, his world-view would probably have stopped at mere cynicism, the nihilistic rejection of meaning, which is quite different from Enlightened Living: nothing has any intrinsic meaning or value, but everything is a form of consciousness. It would be tempting to say that consciousness, therefore, has more value than any of the forms, but that binds consciousness to the relative world. As we've said before, consciousness isn't on any continuum of values, it just is.

In contrast to cynicism, which is separateness, *scepticism* is a healthy questioning in the absence of evidence. Adopting a sceptical view until experience has transformed understanding into wisdom is the path of detachment and it avoids falling into the trap of despondency and cynicism on the one hand or over-excited enthusiasm on the other. Thinking in twos like this will draw you away from an objective third point, which is not somewhere in the middle of the continuum but is quite detached from it.

Real fulfilment doesn't require anything to make it more fulfilling and nothing could be taken from it to make it less so. This isn't the temporary happiness that comes from some passing material thing or the unhappiness when it does pass and is 'lost', but rather the bliss that can't be reduced or added to because it is your own Self. It doesn't depend on anything, mental or physical. This kind of bliss is the peace that passes understanding and can't adequately be described, but most people would recognise a time when they felt quite free of striving, completely content with just being. For most of us, it doesn't take long for the striving to rush in again, which is to be expected because we've become conditioned by the message that is passed from generation to generation:

"Our parents teach us grasping and attachment, giving meaning to things, believing that we exist as a self-entity and that things belong to us. We hear this over and over again and it penetrates our hearts and stays there as our habitual feeling. We're taught to get things, to accumulate and hold on to them, to see them as important and as ours."

(Ajahn Chah: *Everything Arises, Everything Falls Away*)

Consider for a moment what Ajahn Chah is saying: we give meaning and purpose to things, to accumulate and to own things. My house, my car, my wife/husband/partner, my children. The temporary form of our bodies and minds becomes 'my life'; even consciousness becomes 'my attention'. In truth, none of it belongs to anyone. The only meaning things have, we have added to them; they are, in other words, empty. This is what we mean by 'empty' in Enlightened Living. We do not exist as separate selves other than as empty passing forms, subject to time, space and the law of cause and effect; nothing belongs to anyone since there is no one there to own it, just an imagined 'me'.

This is not the emptiness of despondency but is paradoxically fulfilment in emptiness. Ajahn Chah tells the story of the two monks debating why a flag was blowing. One said it was because of the wind, the other that it was because of the flag. This went on until the teacher intervened and said neither was right and that there is no flag and no wind:

"It's all empty – void; empty of flag and empty of wind. In the great emptiness, there is no flag and there is no wind. There is no birth, no old age, no sickness or death. Our conventional

understanding of flag and wind is only a concept. In reality, there is nothing. That's all! There is nothing more than empty labels... When we see and understand with truth, then there is only this great emptiness. It's here that there is no more 'we', no 'they', no 'self' at all."

(Ajahn Chah: *Food for the Heart*)

This is a difficult message and indeed an extremely depressing one if we stop there. One of the reasons people become despondent and depressed is that they go this far but stop short and end up feeling there's no point to it all. We need to start from there, with the view that there is no destiny or purpose. There is no point to it at all, but only if 'it' is something we're striving for in the relative world of uncertain forms. Our everyday experience tells us that nothing has intrinsic meaning. Think back to the last time you were fired up and passionate about achieving something; once achieved, what then? As quickly as possible we add the next thing, so there is no gap between being consumed by the false attribution of meaning to one thing or another. Hard though it may be, we need to start by acknowledging the emptiness of everything if we're to stop chasing after the mirage of meaning and ownership, believing that we exist as a meaningful self and attributing meaning to things that have no meaning.

To do so without falling into one or other of the opposites of happiness or unhappiness requires the third point we described earlier. At some stage in his life, Bob Dylan went through a Christian phase and wrote some songs about it. In one he describes the contrasting fortunes of the many parts we might end up playing in our lives, humble, famous or infamous, but the chorus to each verse is that whatever the part, you always serve somebody. In the song this 'somebody' is either the devil or the Lord, and although he may or may not have said as much, the inspiration for the song must surely have been *Matthew 6:24*,

"No man can serve two masters: for either he will hate the one and love the other; or else he will hold to the one and despise the other.

Ye cannot serve God and mammon."

(*Matthew 6:24*)

The problem with the verse is the same one that besets all religion: the separation between one thing and another, between either God or mammon. Separation is the foundation of ego and must inevitably lead to anger, hatred, guilt and the rest, yet the solution is so simple, which is to adopt the third point of indifference. Indifference is described perfectly in the Zen Buddhist story we used in Chapter 4: the monk in the story responds to all the accusations, demands and subsequent apologies he's subjected to with the same phrase, "Is that so?"

If value and meaning are not attached to anything, then it makes no difference what happens in the endless sequence of cause and effect that is the nature of things. Sometimes the cause is known, sometimes not, but enquiring after causes and effects will not bring enlightenment. Perhaps by behaving in a particular way, you will ascend into heaven or be fully realised and transcend birth and death, perhaps not. But to do anything for a purpose or goal is to be bound to the fruit of action and to be distracted from the present. The present is the only place enlightenment can occur. The rest is imagined and even five minutes ago or five minutes hence comes under the thousand-year rule: whatever happened five minutes ago might as well have been a thousand years ago.

What then about planning? Don't we have to plan? In a limited sense, yes – if you're travelling somewhere you don't just turn up at the airport expecting to get on a flight. These are simple needs that arise all the time in our everyday lives and they range from planning travel to deciding whether or not to take a particular job. All of these decisions and plans involve discriminating mind and even at this simple level, we can see the need for discriminating mind to function clearly. Life is seldom as straightforward as just deciding about one particular course of action or another, but all that has increased is relative complexity; the principle of maintaining a still point from which to decide remains the same. Just responding impulsively or endlessly deliberating in an attempt to arrive at a perfect outcome are equally to do with attachment and will distort our perception.

This is not to say that a decision taken with a clear mind will necessarily turn out to be 'right', but regretting having taken a decision about something yesterday and berating yourself today for having done so simply adds attachments. We encounter any number of opportunities that arise from causes and effects we may have no knowledge of; we take decisions at the time, not by procrastinating or by acting impulsively but by keeping our minds as indifferent as possible and taking the opportunity that seems most appropriate for meeting the need.

Liberation from attachment comes with surrender. You can't easily surrender what you're attached to, but the way to begin is to see attachments for what they are, from the perspective of discriminating mind. This is the third point. Surrender might sound like defeat, but this is again thinking in twos. There isn't anything to surrender to, just a letting go of attachments that have been forged by attributing illusory value and meaning to conditioned habits. Those who are religious will attach a positive value to God and a negative one to mammon and the opposite would be true for those who are attached to the material world.

Returning to Matthew 6:24, the distinction between the opposites of God and mammon might be represented like this:

God < – – – – > mammon

Thinking in twos leaves you no option but to align yourself with one or the other pole of the continuum, or to try to position yourself somewhere in the middle between the two, but there isn't really a neutral point along the continuum. To be neutral or indifferent means moving outside of the continuum to find a point not located somewhere in the middle of the line separating God and mammon, but more like the third point of a triangle:

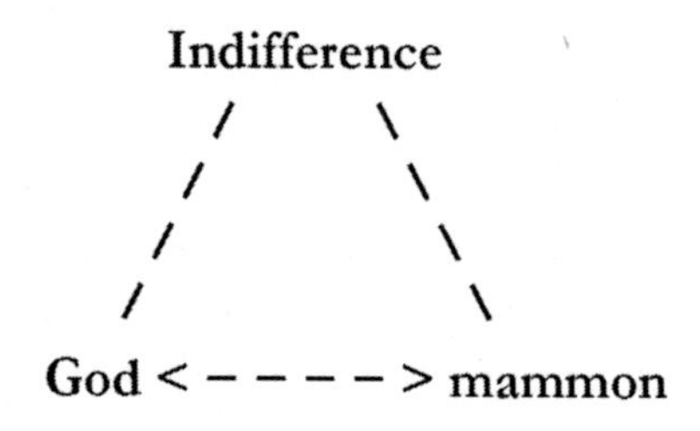

Diagrams like this can be invaluable aids to understanding, but understanding needs to be transformed into wisdom by practice in the world. The practice is to observe and the third point provides a dispassionate vantage point from which to do so. The observer is consciousness; what is observed are the forms of the world, material or subtle.

Our conditioned experience of observing is mostly like attention seeming to beam outwards from a source within ourselves. The trap that this generates is becoming identified with the observer, creating a separation between ourselves and the rest of the world. Although the truth is that both observer and observed are different forms of the same consciousness, this paradox can be acknowledged without becoming entangled in debates about what observes and what is observed. Indeed, we resolved that distraction in Chapters 2 and 3 by quoting from Ajahn Chah, who said that the mind is one thing and the knowing another, even though the knowing originates in the same mind. From the perspective of Enlightened Living, the still point from which observation takes place is discriminating mind uncontaminated by attachments.

What's required is maintaining what Ajahn Chah calls in those quotes a 'watchful eye'. A starting point for watchfulness might be to observe the body, the way that breathing changes when you become tense, for example, but whatever the body does arises first in the mind. Observing the mind is the key to enlightenment. Thoughts are also forms, stories about an imagined world. Once identified and attached, the central character in the story will justify whatever we do. We become by turns all-conquering or all-suffering and, according to ego, justifiably so.

All of this begins innocuously enough as simple conditioning, but often ends in attachment. The question is whether you live a justified life or an examined one. What is examined is the conditioning and the attachments created by the endless sequence of causes and effects. Fed by desire and aversion we develop preferences and there may be a very short step from preference to addiction. What is it that you're unable to respond to with the phrase, 'Is that so?' Examining these attachments doesn't mean analysing them and picking them apart and even less so criticising yourself for developing the attachment. Because nothing has intrinsic value or meaning, there's nothing personal – 'personal' is the view from ego and invites justification.

To go further means discovering what fulfilment really is and this requires recalling the distinction between relative and absolute. The example we used at the beginning of this chapter, being promoted at work, does offer fulfilment, but only of a temporary kind. So too with hunger. As the gap between meals widens, energy is consumed and hunger increases. We then have a meal and there is undoubtedly the fulfilment of a need. We might see an uplifting sight, a sunset perhaps, and there is the fulfilment in the mind of an idea like beauty. It is just an idea – the sunset isn't trying to be beautiful and someone else might not think it beautiful at all. The fulfilment is temporary and limited and is likely to be contaminated by attachments: wistfully remembering the sunset after it has past and longing for the next one. Every day, the sun rises and the sun sets, all a consequence of cause and effect; attributing value to them binds you to regret and longing.

Preferring one food over another is an attachment to a concept, just as attributing 'beauty' to a sunset is simply attributing beauty to something which is neither beautiful nor ugly but just is, quite independent of what we might think of it. Ajahn Chah again:

"You might have a vase. You feel that it is nice, but from its own side, it exists indifferently. It doesn't have anything to say; it is only you who have the feelings about it, you who live and die over it. If you dislike or hate it, it won't be affected. That's your affair. It is indifferent, but you have these feelings of like or dislike and then get attached to them."

(Ajahn Chah: *Everything Arises, Everything Falls Away*)

Attachment comes about when the life is devoted to ego, rather than simply responding to the need. So what is the 'need' to watch a sunset? There isn't one, but the mistake is thinking that meeting needs is performing an action for someone or something, in which case it is no longer meeting a need – paradoxically, needs can only be met indifferently. When a need is really met there is unity, not one separate entity doing something for another separate entity. The absence of measure and the devotion of the life to ego are one and the same. You pass a sweet-smelling rose, the recollection of the scent keeps coming back and you return to smell the rose over and over again. This lack of measure is wanting more and wanting more is greed. Holding onto thoughts is greed. Greed is wanting more for me, which is separation.

None of this means we should stop doing things. There are always needs to be met and sunsets to enjoy in the moment, and there is certainly nothing to be gained from denial. In our earlier example, you may really like chocolate, but rigidly denying yourself chocolate won't lead to freedom from desire and just incurs suffering. Instead, eat the chocolate, but mindfully, so that you know when to stop! Unfortunately, we've come to associate denial with discipline and discipline in turn with enlightenment. Discipline is needed, but discipline isn't a forced process. Take sex as an example. Celibate monks used to whip themselves or wear hair shirts when sexual or other desires arose (perhaps they still do!), mistakenly thinking that they were conquering desire with denial and pain. At the other extreme is indulging a desire like sex, transforming it into an obsessive addiction.

Why is there this overwhelming preoccupation with sex? No doubt the pleasure it gives is part of the explanation, but pleasurable experiences can be enjoyed without addiction. It would be easy to lump all additions together, like drugs, alcohol, food and sex, but there are clear differences: alcohol and many drugs are physically addictive, so the body becomes dependent on having them. Sex is rather more subtle and has become connected with other features of ego, like power – sexual exploitation is almost exclusively of women by men. And why should men so want to demean women, if they were not in some way threatened by them? Ego moves in mysterious ways, but the outcome is always suffering. Where is the man that Hamlet describes, noble in reason, infinite in faculty, in action like an angel? What a falling-off there is when ego acts unchecked by discriminating mind and measure.

Desires and aversions are fuelled and supported by emotion, but just as you can't obliterate desires that arise you can't obliterate the emotion that they depend upon. The real solution is to observe what satisfying these desires brings. Is it really fulfilling? This is just temporary happiness, followed eventually by the desire again. Seeing these things for what they are won't stop them in their tracks, but by letting go of the attachment they will diminish when they're ready to – in other words, when you been able to see them for what they actually are. Measure, which is the theme of Chapter 7, also tells us that there is a time for every purpose. When sexual desire is kindled during puberty, it isn't 'sinful' – all creatures are designed to procreate in some way or another, and the pleasure humans derive from sex is real at the time. To the extent there is sin, it is allowing the desires to so govern the mind that they preoccupy us even when the objects of desire are absent. Addiction takes over and addiction is at the heart of ego.

So, enjoying the temporary fulfilment of the desires of body and mind is not something we need to avoid in order for enlightenment to arise and when there is enlightenment, the conditioned, relative world of preferences doesn't disappear. In Act 2, Scene II of Shakespeare's Twelfth Night, Sir Toby Belch asks Malvolio, "Dost thou think, because thou art virtuous; there shall be no more cakes and ale?" There's a saying that before enlightenment, carry water, chop wood; after enlightenment, carry water, chop wood. As the Buddha himself discovered after trying to starve himself into enlightenment, all he was doing was indulging ego – he'd forgotten to enjoy while not coveting.

Coveting is the addiction to wanting more. Satisfying relative desires does bring a kind of fulfilment, but there is another level of fulfilment which requires neither thoughts nor anything outside of ourselves. Simply satisfying body and mind in a measured way will eventually lead to 'what's next?', but there is a transcendent fulfilment which is complete and it is discovered by surrendering attachments to the fruit of action. Fulfilment of this kind follows from the dissolution of the sense of separateness that ego brings. There is a simple metaphor that describes the contrast between separateness and unity: a trough of water with a barrier inserted in the middle separating the water into two. When the barrier's removed, the apparent separation between the two parts disappears. In the same way, when the obstacles of attachment are surrendered, the consciousness that appears to be within my mind is united with the consciousness that is never absent anywhere. In the book *Be as You Are*,

Ramana Maharshi is asked when suffering will cease; he replies, "Not until individuality is lost."

This is why there is a feeling of oneness or unity when enlightenment arises and the sense of being separate disappears. Separation never, in fact, existed other than as ego, and ego itself doesn't exist as an entity. When enlightenment does arise, the world doesn't stop. The sequence of states, none of which has any intrinsic meaning, continues under the governance of cause and effect, but two kinds of wisdom might arise: because I can observe this endless flow of effects I can't be them and that everything is indeed a form of consciousness. Just telling yourself this is not enough. Wisdom starts with understanding, which is abstract and theoretical, but becomes wisdom when it is practised.

"It means coming to the point where the mind is empty. This doesn't mean that there is nothing, no people or objects in the world. There is empty mind, there are people, there are things. But in the mind there is the perception of it all as truth, as something uncertain."

(Ajahn Chah: *Everything Arises, Everything Falls Away*)

So paradoxically, fulfilment requires indifference, since there isn't anyone or anything becoming fulfilled: separation and enlightenment are irreconcilable and no separate individual can be enlightened. It is sometimes said that enlightenment isn't for everyone; in fact, enlightenment is for no one! Indifference is the third point, the view of the world from discriminating mind and it shows empty forms arising and passing in an endless succession of cause and effect.

Showing that emptiness and fulfilment can be simultaneously one and the same is usually done using paradoxical statements, like asking for the sound of one hand clapping, or Ajahn Chah's flowing water that is at the same time still. We've all experienced the stilling of the mind, which requires going from being in and of the world to a more detached being in the world but not of it. A still mind observing the ever-changing relative states of body and mind is still, flowing water. Understanding it in this way can be helpful, but will remain academic until the mind is actually stilled:

"Creation is neither good nor bad; it is as it is. It is the human mind which puts all sorts of constructions on it, seeing things from its own angle and interpreting them to suit its own interests. A woman is just a woman, but one mind calls her 'mother', another 'sister' and still another 'aunt' and so on. Men love women, hate snakes and are indifferent to the grass and stones by the roadside. These value-judgements are the cause of all the misery in the world. Creation is like a peepal tree: birds come to eat its fruit or take shelter under its branches, people cool themselves in its shade, but some may hang themselves on it. Yet the tree continues to lead its quiet life, unconcerned with and unaware of the uses it is put to."

(Godman (Ed): *Be as You Are – The Teachings of Ramana Maharshi*)

It's like this: when the stories we create in our minds are seen as having no value other than the value we attribute to them, we can take attention from them and they fade away. They're likely to come back, partly as a consequence of simple conditioning but also because we're bound to them by attachment. The fact that they come back is neither here nor there, but by observing them as they enter they can be seen as conditioning or as attachments and the attachments can be surrendered. This is easier than it might seem – when the thought arises, is it dedicated to a separate self? If it isn't and is just remembering to feed the dog, that's conditioning; if it is and is me resentfully having to feed the dog because no one else will bother, that's ego.

Letting go is actually effortless. The effort is in maintaining the identification. Letting go leads to emptiness and if we empty our minds of attachments we don't then need to fill it with consciousness – consciousness was never absent, just captured by attachments. In the Gospel of Thomas, Jesus describes the kingdom of heaven as being like:

(Logion 97) "A woman who was carrying a jar
Full of meal. While she was walking (on a) distant road,
The handle of the jar broke.
The meal streamed out behind her on the road.
She did not know (it), she had noticed no
Accident. After she came into her house,

She put the jar down, she found it empty."

(*The Gospel of Thomas*)

Surrender is letting go of what's treasured in the heart, bound into conserving mind by ego. The parable is just a metaphor, which needn't be elaborated into wondering how she'll feed her children! Emptiness is freedom from the burden of ego and the creation of ways of thinking that are governed by the emotional glue of attachment. Our distant ancestors find one day that the sun gradually disappears in an eclipse. Other animals respond in a conditioned way and simply act as if it were night for a while. Since we associate darkness with danger, we instead imagine an evil spirit that temporarily steals the sun, only to be won over again by the good spirit of light. We end up believing in an invisible world of good and evil spirits influencing our destiny and we're then obliged to protect ourselves by appeasing them in some way. It makes no difference whether there is one God and one Devil or many of each, or whether performing certain rites and behaving in particular ways allows us to escape from hell or avoid reincarnation, the principle is the same and it is all driven by fear.

One of the Upanishads says that fear makes the sun come up and the sun go down, which is a metaphorical expression of the emotion that lies at the heart of attachments: fear. Since everything is constantly in flux and becoming something else there is no certainty, and uncertainty generates not only fear but also the desire to control things – if you think you know what's coming you feel you can prepare yourself. You don't know what's coming, nobody ever does. Which is not an argument for fatalism. We still act, but what are we acting on? Past experience will certainly play a role and might help in dealing with the current situation, but it may not – conditioning is mechanical and it can limit the way you respond.

The world is a succession of empty forms, but they are all forms of a single consciousness. Just like mindfulness, the question of fulfilment is what are these empty forms filled with? Ignorance is a mind full of egotistical thoughts and actions devoted to things that never satisfy. Surrender these attachments and the mind is filled with consciousness, because it is never absent. Actions can then be performed from the still point of discriminating mind, meeting the need but with nothing added. None of this happens except in the present and having presence of mind means responding to what's actually in front of you at the time, being both empty and fulfilled.

Chapter 6
Meditation

The word 'meditation' often evokes ideas that tie it to one or another spiritual tradition, with all the associated rituals: sitting in a lotus position, burning incense and all the rest. This can deter people from enquiring any further, which is a shame. Stripped of all of the spiritual mumbo-jumbo, meditation is an extremely simple practice that involves controlling attention, focussing consciousness on just one thing to the exclusion of everything else. That's all it is, but the consequence of doing so is that your active, moving mind becomes still:

"When the mind is still, it's in its natural, unadulterated state. As soon as the mind moves, it becomes conditioned. When the mind is attracted to something, it becomes conditioned. When aversion arises, it becomes conditioned. The desire to move here and there arises from conditioning. If our awareness doesn't keep pace with these mental proliferations as they occur, the mind will chase after them and be conditioned by them."

(Ajahn Chah – *Food for the Heart*)

We've talked a lot about conditioning in previous chapters, where we said that it is not of itself a problem – in fact, it is impossible to have no conditioning. The problem is when we become attached to the object of conditioning. It can be confusing when teachers like Ajahn Chah talk about conditioning as something to be avoided, but the confusion is simply a reflection of differences in the way words are used. Self-evidently, conditioning is not only unavoidable but actually useful. The trap that Ajahn Chah is alluding to here is mechanical practice, and with meditation, it is a trap that's easy to fall into.

Innumerable studies of the effects of meditation have shown that there are significant benefits for health and well-being, but these too can be a distraction. Meditating is then done as a means to an end, rather than an end in itself. There may be benefits from meditation and doing it in order to live longer may be one of them, but of what significance is that? Suppose you could know – and it isn't possible to know – that the times you spent meditating added 5 years to your life. So what? Eventually, everyone dies; the real question is what will you do between now and then. The length of any life is irrelevant. We might then say that it is the quality of the life that counts rather than how long it might last, but 'quality of life' is ordinarily defined in material, relative terms: the quality of *my* life. What really counts is whether consciousness is made available through the life, moment to moment, without any claims being made on it. Above any other practice, meditation allows this to happen; meditating to achieve something will have the opposite effect:

"The end of meditation is meditation itself. The search for something through and beyond meditation is end-gaining, and that which is gained is again lost. Seeking a result is the continuation of self-projection; the result, however lofty, is the projection of desire."

(Krishnamurti: *Commentaries on Living Series* I)

Meditation helps to establish mindfulness, making you less subject to the antics of a mind that is always elsewhere, conjuring up worlds that never existed. All of these stories concocted in the mind are centred on ego and meditation is really about discovering how to remove ego. Putting Ajahn Chah's earlier quote into the context of Enlightened Living, it is the stories we chase after that need to be addressed rather than habitual conditioning. Once ego has been dissolved actions become conscious, whether they are habitual or not. As we will see in Chapter 7, at any given moment there is a choice, either to act for oneself or to remove oneself from the action and allow it to happen. Meditation provides an explicit and systematic practice for getting oneself out of the way and becoming nobody, a passer-by. No wonder ego objects!

Meditation doesn't involve suffering, so the first thing is that you don't need to sit in a lotus position. Some people find that useful, but it is in no way a prerequisite – a comfortable chair works just as well. Much has been written about the beneficial effects of a lotus position for aligning centres described as chakras. These are said to run up your spine to the top of your head and meditation is supposed to be aided when they are aligned. Sitting reasonably upright allows for much easier breathing and is undoubtedly helpful; there may or may not be chakras, but speculating about them is just another distraction and has no practical benefit. It is best not to lie down, mainly because during meditation your body will be relaxed and by a simple association, being relaxed and lying down will often lead to sleep. Meditation isn't sleeping, though even experienced meditators will sometimes drop off. All that means is that you're tired and you need to rest, so if you're trying to meditate and just keep nodding off, go have a nap and return to it later.

The next thing is that there isn't a fixed time in the day that you 'ought' to meditate or a fixed length of time that you ought to meditate for. We tend to be more wakeful in the morning and morning and evening are propitious to the extent that we've not yet started work or have finished for the day, but there isn't anything spiritually special about those times. It does usually take a while for the mind to settle and half-an-hour does seem to be the optimal time for meditation, but especially when you first begin, that can seem a long time! There's no point in forcing yourself, that's just suffering.

When you first start, a useful strategy is to set a small alarm for say 10 minutes and leave it outside the door. When it goes off, if all you've been doing is struggling to still your mind, stop at that point and try again the next day. With practice, you should find that you're comfortable to continue after the alarm has sounded, particularly if your mind has become relatively free of its seemingly incessant activity, so then just continue until it feels natural to stop. The key is to practice regularly – an ideal is twice a day for about 30 minutes, but don't set this as a goal! Just work from where you are, without any expectations, requirements or mystical speculations.

Anything worthwhile requires practice and discipline, but as we've said many times, discipline should not be confused with suffering. So what does meditation involve? Begin by choosing a comfortable chair, preferably one that will allow you to sit with a straight spine and find a position on the chair that you'll be able to maintain for the full period of the practice. Lean into the back of the chair if that helps – remember that this isn't a military exercise. If your legs are crossed you will be inhibiting blood circulation to your feet and you'll need to move around sooner, so have your feet flat on the floor. In the same way, having your arms folded is usually less comfortable, so have your arms loose and supported by your thighs with your hands loose in your lap – no need for mystical hand positions. Look around before you begin, so that when you close your eyes you're not wondering about your surroundings. You might prefer to sit outside, in which case become familiar with where you're sitting, though remember that intermittent birdsong or breezes can also become a distraction.

What arises in meditation is an inner peace which in fact is always available and is not dependent on a quiet environment – you can meditate anywhere once you've established the practice, and insisting on a particular chair in a particular spot before you can meditate is just ego at work again. Here are three quotes from very different sources which will help to put this into perspective, one a Roman emperor-statesman and another a Buddhist teacher, and the third from the Vedic tradition:

"Men are continually seeking retreats for themselves, in the country or by the Sea or among the hills... Yet all this is the surest folly, for it is open to thee, every hour, to retire into thyself. And where can a man find a calmer, more restful haven than in his own soul?"

(Marcus Aurelius – *Meditations*)

"Once the mind has let go of external objects, you will no longer feel disturbed by the sound of traffic or other noises. You won't feel irritated with anything outside... they won't be a source of disturbance because the mind won't be paying attention to them as it becomes centred upon the breath."

(Ajahn Chah – *Being Dharma*)

"During meditation, the distracting noises seem very harsh, but if one expands oneself so as to cover everything, then these distractions become very minor things, for they are part of yourself. One would notice them but is not disturbed."

(Shantanand Saraswati – *Good Company*)

Again, it isn't helpful to conjure up ideas about what is being said. We often hear enlightenment described as becoming one with everything and certainly, there is a dissolving of the sense of separation, but the sounds you hear or the things you can see remain forms that are separate from your form. What unity means is acknowledging that all of the forms are forms of the same single consciousness, but that can't be understood by using concepts in the mind. So let's keep it simple and practical: what Shantanand Saraswati means by 'expanding oneself' is allowing the sounds to happen, incorporating them into listening rather than seeing them as interfering with the practice.

Once you feel comfortable, close your eyes. What you're doing is excluding the very vivid and distracting sense of sight and you can then take the first step in controlling your attention by giving it intentionally to the physical sensations you're feeling. Be aware of the weight of your feet on the floor. Feel the weight of your body on the chair and the pressure of your clothes against your skin. Be aware of your breathing; take a deep breath first if you feel that you need to, then just relax your chest and stomach and allow each breath to come and go without any effort.

A lot of tension collects around the point where your neck and shoulders meet, so just let all of that tension go: relax your arms and your hands, then your neck, your scalp and your face. You can think of it as a kind of gate that becomes tightly shut when you're tense; relaxing these muscles opens the gate and allows circulation to flow freely. Let all tension go from around your eyes, your mouth and your jaw and with each out-breath, let any remaining tension dissolve. Don't try to breathe more deeply or more shallowly, but progressively with each gentle out-breath, allow the first gate to open fully.

Next, shift your attention to the rest of your body. You might think about another 'gate' being located in your pelvis, which is opened by relaxing the muscles in your stomach, then extending that to your legs and feet. Feel the weight of your feet on the floor and again with each out-breath, let the tension in your body dissolve away. As you relax, make sure you don't end up slouching – retain enough muscle tension to remain effortlessly upright. A good way to get a sense of what's needed is to notice a baby's posture when it first begins to sit up, balanced and with only sufficient tension to maintain that position, but make sure you continue to be comfortable. Sometimes people try to relax by progressively tensing up muscle groups and then relaxing them, but this is not generally useful because you're introducing tension where there might be none at all and especially with short muscle groups like your hands and forearms the tension can then be even harder to release. Make it simple: start with whatever tension you discover in your body and without adding to it, go from there to gradually releasing it.

Once your body is relaxed but upright the next step is to control your mind. A helpful way to start is to be aware of any sounds you can hear. They can suddenly seem very loud but they haven't changed; all that is happening is that the sounds are reverberating in a mind that has become more still. The sounds themselves may provoke associations that have resulted from conditioning, naming a bird you can hear, for example, or conjuring up a picture of the bird in your mind. They may equally provoke opposition if the sounds are seen as an irritating distraction. Try instead just resting your attention on any sounds you can hear, gradually surrendering the opposition as well as the interest in them.

As you become accustomed to the sounds your mind will be less inclined to be drawn away by them, but mind can't be removed from the process: the associations and the opposition are both formed in the mind, provoked by the sounds and the effects will continue even when the sounds have passed or are no longer heard as loud or irritating. The real challenge is controlling and stilling the mind and it is easy to then put a great effort into trying to force attention away from the thoughts. We often associate control with force, but trying to force thoughts out of your mind usually has the opposite effect of strengthening them.

All of these thoughts will have ego, 'me', at their heart. They are an endless source of entertainment for ego and what feeds and sustains thoughts is giving attention to them. What is needed is something other than the thoughts to rest your attention on, something that is repetitious and contains nothing that would entertain ego. This might be a mantra, which is a word that is repeated in the mind, or breathing. Like chakras much is said about mantras and how they have special powers, but in fact, you can use any word at all: sock will do, or butter, or flower. Traditionally a mantra might be a Sanskrit word and it can be helpful if you don't know the language – butter or sock are much more likely to conjure up pictures of the objects in your mind.

What's important, though, is that you repeat the word and keep your attention on the word alone. Given the associations that come with words you may find focusing on your breathing easier, since it is already repeating of its own accord – rest your attention on the cool sensation in your nose as you breathe in and the warm sensation as you breathe out. Having eyes closed is recommended because it removes visual stimulation, but you can meditate with eyes open and focused on an object, a flower for example. The process is the same: the flower you see will at first generate interest, or speculation about how beautiful it is, etc., but gradually it is seen for what it is – a form of consciousness, with no intrinsic value or meaning other than what we attribute to it. Just as with focusing on breathing, the flower then just is and attention can rest on it without evoking stories about it.

Resting your attention on something like this provides the opportunity to allow all of the frenetic activity, conjuring up the imagined worlds of what you did yesterday and need to do today and tomorrow, to die away. But what happens then? Typically, your mind decides this is far too boring and races off back into the world of imagination! Be prepared: this will inevitably happen. We described in Chapter 3 an aspect of mind which we called moving mind and this is exactly what it does: if you don't give it something to attend to, it will go off and find something. There is nothing wrong with moving mind and it comes into its own in situations like life-or-death emergencies. In these circumstances, people might be caught by the emotion and simply freeze, but when people have presence of mind, their moving mind flies back and forth at incredible speed, collecting information and translating it into appropriate action. When you try to become still, moving mind follows its nature and looks about for something to be stimulated by. Meditation is the opportunity to allow it to come to rest, so as soon as you realise your mind has wandered, bring your attention gently back to whatever technique you're using, such as the object, the repeating word or the in-and-out breath.

Don't be deterred by how much your attention wants to go off and don't put any force into bringing it back – just lead your attention back to the word or to breathing. Given time your mind will begin to settle until all there is in your conscious awareness is the repeating word, the alternating cool and warm sensation of your breath, or the objective form of a flower. In essence, this is all that meditation is – surrendering the endless story-telling in the mind. It is only ego that finds any of these endlessly repeated stories interesting. We want to know what other people are thinking, especially about us, but what's running in someone else's mind is none of your business. What's running in your mind is none of your business either – it isn't of any consequence and for the most part is just babble. Try giving a verbal running commentary on what's passing through your mind; we're endlessly interested in our own chatter, but anyone listening would be bored to tears.

There is a stage beyond the mind becoming still and just resting on the repeating word or the in-and-out breath when all thoughts seem to evaporate – there really is nothing in the mind at all. We'll call this *deep meditation*, where there is no sense of a separate individual being aware of anything. Whatever it is you've used to rest attention on has done its work and is no longer needed:

> *"The mantra is not unity, it only leads to unity where the world of division has no validity. In deep meditation we don't even appreciate the peace, truth, bliss or consciousness; we in fact become peaceful, truthful and blissful."*
>
> (Shantanand Saraswati: *Good Company*).

It is impossible to recall anything about deep meditation since there wasn't an experiencer there at the time. If you can give an account of the state of deep meditation, it didn't happen! However, as with all of the practices described in this book, it is important to not set up deep meditation as a goal – it might or might not occur, especially in the early stages of practice. Any practice of stilling the mind, no matter how deep it might become, is part of Enlightened Living, so begin by just maintaining attention to the repeating word or breath or object, letting all other thoughts dissolve and see where it leads. Here's another description of meditation from Shantanand Saraswati, based on repeating a mantra:

"One starts the mantra and repeats the mantra. One initiates this at the level of the individual and then this repetition of the mantra leads on to the bare thread of meditation. Although it is known as the 'practice of meditation', yet this practice is leading towards the end of all activity. Slowly and gradually this march towards non-activity takes place until one reaches the realm of unity and stillness. This is the experience of Self as universal; here there is no duality and there remains no place to move on to and there is no time to change to for Self is the place, the time and also the substance. In that profound silence, stillness or union all movements stop; there is only 'One without second'."

(*Good Company*)

However deep the meditation, people who practice it will usually describe afterwards a sense of expansion and freedom from the endless and exhausting preoccupation with myself. This is what liberation is. The world of forms doesn't disappear but is seen clearly from the perspective of the third point of conscious discriminating mind, relatively uncontaminated by ego. This is what you truly are. Next time you wake up from a daydream and step back from the imagined drama be aware of the hero/villain/victim that's been created. Do you really think you're one of these characters you imagine in your mind?

These imaginings are relative states, all of them second-hand. The real thing is now, which is why meditation is so important. It shows us what we are: enduring, peaceful consciousness which is not attached to anything at all. This also happens in deep sleep: we have no recollection of anything from deep sleep, but we wake up really refreshed. Meditation is not sleep, and the difference between them can be shown using measures of brain activity, but more importantly we need to discover the difference ourselves, by practising meditation and seeing what arises afterwards.

We need to develop the habit of meditation, but equally we need to guard against mechanical habit becoming a substitute for the practice. Watch the mind as you prepare to meditate: has it become a mechanical process? Once this happens the freshness of the present has been lost. Watch the process of insisting on the one and only chair you can meditate in, of finding a comfortable position to practice, or of the pleasurable expectation of closing your eyes and shutting out the visual world. Closing our eyes is a means to an end, not an end in itself. It is important to be comfortable and sitting on a chair which is more conducive is entirely appropriate, but you can actually meditate anywhere and on most chairs. Once mechanicalness creeps in, habit has replaced practice. It might be useful to not even think or speak about it as meditation, since the word itself has so many connotations. In fact, don't speak about it at all, just do it.

The next step is to be aware of what happens after each practice. We open our eyes and return, as it were, to the relative world, so do we just dive straight back in and lose ourselves in egotism again? Ego is the separate 'me' that we seem to be, but what we describe as 'me' is a temporary, conditioned form. The forms are indeed separate, but what is forgotten is that everyone and everything is a form of the same consciousness. It is impossible to know this by thinking about it but meditation provides the clearest insight into it, not during the actual practice but in the effect afterwards. The most obvious effect is the ease with which attachments can be seen, which is not surprising – discriminating mind can function with much greater clarity when the agitation has subsided. Meditation is a contrived process, sitting by oneself with eyes closed, but this isolation paradoxically leads to an acknowledgement of unity. This is what being one with someone means: not the illusory oneness that comes with being passionately 'in love', but the acknowledgement of consciousness which is the same, despite differences in form.

We can't practice meditation constantly. Liberation can't be confined only to those times when we practice it and in deep meditation, there is, in any case, no individual perception of anything at all. The challenge is to maintain the sense of unity and clarity that remains as an echo, by continuing to be aware of the consciousness that unites us as we go about our daily lives rather than focusing only on the forms which separate us.

Regular meditation supports the everyday practice of mindfulness and is strengthened by allowing the mind to become still as often as we remember and resting awareness on whatever is happening at the time. This doesn't mean having to stop acting. Everything, from just sitting to escaping a disaster, can be done with either a still or an agitated mind and we can continue to observe actions even while we're engaged in them. Mind can be full of thoughts about our next holiday, or about the argument we had with someone yesterday, or it can just be filled with consciousness. Since it can't overflow or be depleted it doesn't need to be topped up in any way. It is never absent. Our minds remain full of consciousness, even when we're in deep sleep or meditating, but what so often happens is that it gets captured and masked by attachments

We usually associate meditation with sitting and with our eyes closed. The Buddha said meditation is not just sitting but also walking, standing and lying down, but he didn't mean being in a state of deep meditation all the time. What he meant was establishing mindfulness in all situations. Deep meditation establishes the foundation for a still mind, but once the eyes are open again the path into meditation is reversed: the relative world returns, offering endless opportunities to re-establish attachments. To help counter this you can try practising meditation in the way the Buddha suggested. Lying down we usually associate with sleep and that may well happen when we try to practice lying down, especially if we close our eyes. Walking meditation precludes sleepiness, but is challenging because the eyes are open: the world is available and the mind will want to elaborate and develop a relationship with the thoughts about what is seen. This is why it is different from 'going for a walk'. Instead, the walking is to and fro, from one point to another and then back again. Ajahn Chah offers a way to visualise it:

"Take a glass and place it on a table for two minutes. When the time is up, place the glass somewhere else on the table for two minutes. Then put it back where you first had it, again for

two minutes. Keep doing that. Do it again and again until you start to suffer, until you doubt until wisdom arises: 'What am I doing, moving a glass back and forth like a madman?' The mind will think in its habitual way. It doesn't matter what anyone says. Just keep moving that glass. Every two minutes, okay? – don't daydream, two minutes not five. As soon as two minutes are up then move it back. Focus on that.

(Walking meditation) isn't just strolling along in a perfunctory way, thinking about this and that for one length of the path. Keep doing it until you're fed up and then see how far that laziness goes. Keep looking until you come to the end of laziness. Whatever it is you experience, you have to go all the way through it before you overcome it."

(*Food for the Heart*)

To try walking meditation find a spot to start from, which might be inside or outside. Don't debate about it, but make sure there is a clear path in front of you. Then walk a few steps, turn around and return to the original spot. Then turn around and repeat the process. It doesn't matter how fast or slowly you walk, or how many steps you take – find out what this is about by practising it. Just as with sitting meditation, the mind conjures up all sorts of ideas about how far I should walk, what's supposed to happen next, etc. This is the 'becoming fed up' that Ajahn Chah refers to. So just as with sitting meditation, try not to identify with what arises, just observe it; then take attention back to walking. Be aware of the sound and feel of each footfall, the change in the air as you turn and just keep going. Walking meditation is done with the eyes open, connected with the world but with the same opportunity that there always is in each moment, either to identify or to witness.

During walking meditation, we remain connected with the world, but without latching on to any of the associations that arise in the mind from our conditioning. Deep meditation is reserved for the sitting form of the practice when the eyes are closed and there is no need to be aware of the world around us. All of the forms of meditation, whether walking, standing, sitting or lying down, are contrived, but they provide a direct experience of peace of mind and freedom from attachments, which is what enlightenment is. With sustained practice, that frame of mind arises in whatever activity we're engaged in and we become what we truly are:

> *"TRUTH is within ourselves; it takes no rise*
> *From outward things, whate'er you may believe.*
> *There is an inmost centre in us all,*
> *Where truth abides in fullness; and around,*
> *Wall upon wall, the gross flesh hems it in,*
> *This perfect, clear perception—which is truth.*
> *A baffling and perverting carnal mesh*
> *Binds it, and makes all error: and, to KNOW,*
> *Rather consists in opening out a way*
> *Whence the imprisoned splendour may escape,*
> *Than in effecting entry for a light*
> *Supposed to be without."*

(Robert Browning – from *Paracelsus 102*)

Chapter 7
Measure and Choice

Measure is a common theme in the Bible, most explicitly in *Ecclesiastes 3*:

1. To everything there is a season and a time to every purpose under heaven:
2. A time to be born and a time to die; a time to plant and a time to pluck up that which is planted;
3. A time to kill and a time to heal; a time to break down and a time to build up;
4. A time to weep and a time to laugh; a time to mourn and a time to dance;
5. A time to cast away stones and a time to gather stones together; a time to embrace and a time to refrain from embracing;
6. A time to get and a time to lose; a time to keep and a time to cast away;
7. A time to rend and a time to sew; a time to keep silence and a time to speak;
8. A time to love and a time to hate; a time of war and a time of peace.

The verse, with its times for killing, getting and hating as well as healing and dancing make it clear that it isn't a prescription for how we should behave. Rather, it is saying that all of these things do occur – this is what happens in the relative world, governed by the chain of causes and effects and mostly under the sway of ego. It also comes from the Old Testament and describes a world dominated by a God very capable of vengeful anger. The message of the New Testament, by contrast, is the gospel of love, not conventional 'love' but indifferent and unconditional love:

"Ye have heard that it hath been said; Thou shalt love thy neighbour and hate thine enemy.

But I say unto you, Love your enemies, bless them that curse you, do good to them that hate you and pray for them which despitefully use you and persecute you."

(*Matthew 5:43–44*)

The idea of a perfect world is a powerful one, but it presents a false hope because ego is ubiquitous – there will always be those who hate and persecute others. However, there will also always be those who choose the opposite and the struggle between forces portrayed as good and evil is an enduring theme of the human condition. The difficulty in casting them as opposites in this way is the same one we encountered in Chapter 5, between God and mammon, which we reconciled not by seeking a point midway between them but rather by adopting a third point which is indifferent to both. The issue is not how to rid the world of ignorance but rather how you respond to it when it occurs and one temptation is to respond in kind, eye for eye and tooth for tooth. This is Old Testament again and amounts to one ego collaborating with another.

Instead, Jesus urges his disciples to do just the opposite, but what does it mean to 'love' and to 'bless' your enemies? The ideal world implicit in the quote is the heaven of God. Loving and blessing your enemies is the sole prerogative of God, expressed through devout believers who are merely instruments of God's work. The love expressed by a devotee in this way can be powerful and redeeming, but it has a flipside: religious intolerance and conflicts are fuelled by the same devotion, expressed as separateness. The problem is that these ideas of good and evil are rooted in the opposites of love and hatred and devotees tread a wavering path between them. How many Christians do you know who behave as Jesus urged them to? I've known many who seek forgiveness week after week for transgressions committed week after week, in a self-perpetuating cycle of guilt and relief.

The view from Enlightened Living is different. Perhaps there is heaven and hell, but the aim of behaving in a conscious, mindful way isn't to avoid one and attain the other. Consciousness is not a judgemental and controlling power. Confession is atonement for past wrongs, seeking forgiveness in the hope of heaven in the future. Conscious, mindful behaviour happens now and it requires adopting the indifferent third point provided by discriminating mind. Enlightened love has the indifference of equanimity, choosing to meet whatever happens with the same response as the Zen monk in Chapter 4: 'Is that so?'

We will return to what unconditional love really means in Chapter 9, but the two quotations at the beginning of this chapter illustrate not only the difference between the Old and New Testaments but also between relative and absolute. The world of Ecclesiastes 3 is the relative one, where measure holds sway. Saying that there is a time for everything is as much about probability as it is about duration: the events it describes will happen in due course and will last for a time, determined by measure. The world of Matthew 5 is absolute, giving with no expectation of getting anything in return. What compromises the message is that the giving usually does include an expectation of the love being reciprocated, either here now or in the reward of ascending to heaven. There is an implicit judgement of how others behave. Enlightened Living would say that the way other people act is none of your business; what counts is how you respond. The only thing you're answerable to is the wisdom afforded by your own discriminating mind.

Consciousness is measureless and is the same everywhere. In deep sleep and in deep meditation the sense of time and space – and hence also measure – are suspended and the unity that arises is known only retrospectively by the feeling that is left afterwards. The relative world is locked into time and space: even in dreams everything has a beginning, a middle and an end, so everything, whether physical or subtle, has a duration. This might be measured in millionths of a second or billions of years, but each form begins, exists for a period of time and ends.

For some things, the duration can be observed and known and even changed – for example, you can decide to hold your breath and hence change the duration of that particular breath.

You could even choose to bring 'your life' to an end. None of this changes measure, since measure is a function of cause and effect. If you decide to hold your breath, that's the cause, and the effect is that the breath is retained longer. You can't hold your breath indefinitely, so doing it will illustrate very clearly what is meant by measure, but why would you want to hold your breath? Having control in this way seems to break the law of cause and effect which underpins measure, but the control is illusory. The form that you are now had a beginning, will exist for a time and will surely pass. The more important question, which we've already posed, is, what will you devote the remaining life to?

The relative world is lawful at every level and science is about discovering these laws that govern the material world. As knowledge has advanced the laws have been found to be more and more subtle, and at the quantum level involve probability and uncertainty rather than mechanical causation, but they remain laws and there is no choice, as we understand the concept, to step outside of the laws of nature: they make tigers behave like tigers, irrespective of where they are. There may be some differences between individual tigers, what we would call 'personality' in humans and as we move higher up the evolutionary tree the differences between individuals become more marked. However, we can only speculate about what really goes on in a gorilla's mind and it isn't relevant to living as an enlightened human being anyway. The real field of our endeavours is where each of us finds ourselves: what we are and what our lives are devoted to.

Laws do vary, depending for the most part on whether they are either ordained by physics, chemistry, and biology, or are man-made. Things are rather different in the quantum realm but within the confines of the known, relative universe, physical laws allow predictions to be made about the effects of particular causes. Man-made laws are a function of culture – there were no traffic-lights prior to the invention of motor vehicles – and they can be evaded. There are simple observations to be made about these laws and the effects of ignoring them, such as driving through a red traffic light. Disobeying rules of the road will be a consequence of either attention being captured or the force of ego and the latter case clearly involves both choice and an absence of measure: the traffic light will go green again, but we run the red traffic light because of self-serving ego.

Somewhere between physical and social laws are those governing the process of conditioning. Expressed simply, conditioning is developing habitual behaviours to seek what we like and avoid what we dislike, but there is an element of choice involved and our preferences do sometimes change over time. Whatever the nature of the laws involved, though, at the heart of law is cause and effect: everything is an effect of a prior cause and will, in turn, become the cause of an effect to follow. Hunger will continue to arise and persist until the need is met by eating, but we might be so driven by a desire that we choose to eat too much and then suffer the consequences. A familiar example is choosing to make ourselves unhappy by entertaining miserable thoughts in our minds. Thoughts are much more subtle and negative thoughts, in particular, tend to keep recurring. What keeps drawing them back into the mind is ego, but when they recur there is a choice either to pursue them or to surrender them.

Think back to the last time you had a heated argument with someone: afterwards, how often did you continue to conjure up the incident in your mind, usually with you winning the argument or saying all of the things you afterwards wished you'd said at the time? All of this is devoted to trying to retrieve a perceived loss of self-esteem and only ego needs to justify itself. Having churned it over and over for a couple of weeks, maybe you went back to the person to try to get some closure, only to find they didn't even remember the incident! Or we might just get fed up with this endless ruminating about how upset we're choosing to make ourselves and our inclination then might be to try to obliterate or fight the thoughts. It can be frustrating and dispiriting when they keep coming back, but they will stop, provided you don't continue to feed them with attention whenever they do return.

The length of time that these thoughts last is their measure, after which they cease. After all, you will probably struggle to recall something that a year ago completely preoccupied your mind with negative thoughts. The more attached you are to the thoughts and what they represent the longer you will continue to feed them with attention and the longer they will last: ego distorts measure. With thoughts and their associated habitual behaviours, their tenacity also depends on the degree of emotion that accompanies them – as we saw in Chapter 4, the more intense the emotion, the stronger the attachment, which is why thoughts about traumatic personal events are likely to remain permanently lodged somewhere in memory. This doesn't mean that people who've suffered trauma will never be free of the emotion it provokes. Although the thoughts will recur, the emotional response that comes with them can be surrendered. They've then exhausted their emotional measure, effectively leaving just an empty thought.

The sequence of cause and effect might be positive or negative, good or bad, but these are just values that we attribute to things. The values are determined by ego and one of the consequences is that we often end up trying to circumvent the law of cause and effect in order to obtain what most suits us. This is why ego distorts measure. Attachment to anything, material or subtle, will lead to it remaining beyond its measure. And the way to avoid this is to follow the principles of Enlightened Living: to cultivate indifference and to surrender. There is a degree of acceptance required here. Angry thoughts might well arise and although anger is separation and ignorance, the attachment is compounded by berating yourself for feeling angry. If it arises, observe it as soon as you can and let it pass. How anyone else behaves is not relevant – the measure of anger isn't the anger in others, but its duration on our minds.

The choice here is between justifying an egotistical response or seeing it for what it is, a passing state. Observation offers the opportunity to be indifferent to it – in other words, when something happens that we don't like, that's no different from something happening that we do like. To act with indifference in this way means knowing measure: that every form arises, lasts for a while and then ends, but has no intrinsic value or meaning:

Prospero: "… the gorgeous palaces,
The solemn temples, the great globe itself,
Yea, all which it inherit, shall dissolve
And, like this insubstantial pageant faded,
Leave not a rack behind. We are such as stuff
As dreams are made on and our little life
Is rounded with a sleep."
(William Shakespeare: *The Tempest, Act 4 Scene I*)

Without measure, liberation is impossible. It isn't a practice to try out from time to time, it is the very heart of practice. When Hamlet is presented with the challenge to a duel with Laertes, he tells Horatio how uneasy he feels in his heart. Horatio replies that if his mind dislikes anything, it should be obeyed and he seeks to prevent Hamlet from entering the duel by making an excuse for him. Hamlet disagrees: "If it be now, 'tis not to come; if it be not to come, it will be now; if it be not now, yet it will come; the readiness is all" (William Shakespeare: *Hamlet, Act 5 Scene I*). Hamlet speaks from the heart, Horatio from reason, but as a consequence of cause and effect, the tragic end to the play will come, one way or another. In *Twelfth Night*, Malvolio's insult to Feste proves his undoing; in the final scene Feste describes the inexorable sequence of cause and effect that led to Malvolio's humiliation: "And thus the whirligig of time brings in his revenges" (William Shakespeare: *Twelfth Night, Act 5 Scene I*).

Hamlet's 'readiness' is like the constant vigilance that Shantanand Saraswati described as a necessary condition for sustaining enlightenment: not a fearful wakefulness, just watching the mind. Shantanand Saraswati describes the failure of measure as being naturally attracted to things we come into contact with, but not knowing when to stop. This doesn't just apply to the obvious things like food or drink, but also to our senses, such as not knowing when to stop looking or hearing. We stop to enjoy the scent of a rose but want to keep going back for more. We see a sunset and feel disappointment when darkness encroaches on it. We 'fall in love' with someone and become completely preoccupied with thoughts about that person. What has arisen is addiction, craving:

"When we undertake to train the mind to be at peace with every situation, in the beginning when a defiled emotion comes up, the mind won't be peaceful. It's going to be distracted and out of control. Why? Because there's craving... Craving not to experience something, craving to be at peace, craving not to be distracted and agitated –it's all craving."

(Ajahn Chah: *Food for the Heart*)

Ajahn Chah also urges constant vigilance, saying that the mind gets entangled in emotions, but wherever it strays we need to keep what he calls a 'watchful eye'. He compares it to raising water buffaloes:

"You've got the farmer, some rice plants and the water buffalo. Now the water buffalo, it wants to eat those plants... Your mind is the water buffalo. Defiled emotions are like the rice plants. The knowing is the farmer... When tending a water buffalo, what do you do? You release it, allowing it to wander freely, but you keep a close eye on it. If it strays too close to the rice plants, you yell out. When the buffalo hears, it backs away... But don't get caught taking a siesta. If you lie down and doze off, those rice plants will be history. Dharma practice is the same: you watch over your mind; the knowing tends the mind."

(Ajahn Chah: *Food for the Heart*)

Watchfulness and vigilance do require discipline, but as we saw in Chapters 4 and 5, true discipline is not effortful. Shantanand Saraswati described discipline as 'moving freely', which comes from surrendering attachments. What could be more effortful than sustaining the addictions of attachment? Discipline is remembering to observe, to be mindful; when discriminating mind is clouded, conditioning becomes transformed into attachment. Measure gives a clear indication of how to practice becoming 'passers-by'. Noticing the sweet scent of the rose is a conditioned response resulting from our attribution of sweetness to it. The scent itself is also a result of conditioning: the sweet scent attracts insects and has arisen through the conditioning process of evolution.

Appreciating the scent when we become aware of it doesn't of itself incur attachment. Trying to remain aloof from conditioned responses is a distortion of discipline, an effortful denial that contradicts the simple enjoyment encouraged by the Isha Upanishad we quoted from in Chapter 4. The next line from that Upanishad reminds us, though, to not covet or claim the enjoyment. Walking down a street where there is a rose in bloom the scent spreads out over a few metres, and while you're in the scent cloud, enjoy; once you've passed, surrender it. Claiming it would be to return again and again to the rose, hankering after the scent. This is attachment and addiction, so just pass by. Measure is regulated by surrender.

One way to understand measure is to notice the difference between needs and wants, which we described in Chapter 5. What do we really need? Needs might be seen as requirements, such as food, water and air. Wants, on the other hand, are desires, the acquisition of things that enhance how ego feels and is seen by others. Under the sway of ego these desires become addictions, and the addictions of attachment lead to insatiably wanting more. As Ajahn Chah said, he didn't know any rich people, only people who wanted more and it doesn't apply only to material things. We want more power, more control, more fame; even, paradoxically, more misery.

The distinction between needs and wants can become rather blurred and it is important not to allow it to devolve into the false discipline of denial. Knowing the difference between needs and wants is about knowing the true measure of things, knowing how much is enough. Actions continue, but they're performed without longing for the chore to end, or becoming addicted to what you're doing and being unwilling to stop. These are both an absence of measure. Nisargadatta Maharaj was asked whether enlightenment meant giving up all action and his answer reflects the essence of measure in Enlightened Living:

"Not at all. There will be marriage, there will be children, there will be earning money to maintain a family; all this will happen in the natural course of events, for destiny must fulfil itself; you will go through it without resistance, facing tasks as they come, attentive and thorough, both in small things and big. But the general attitude will be of affectionate detachment, enormous goodwill, without expectation of return, constant giving without asking. In marriage you are neither the husband

nor the wife; you are the love between the two. You are the clarity and kindness that makes everything orderly and happy... You realise that the person you became at birth and will cease to be at death is temporary and false. You are not the sensual, emotional and intellectual person, gripped by desires and fears. Find out your real being. 'What am I?' is the most fundamental question of all philosophy..."

(Nisargadatta Maharaj: *I Am That*)

The mistaken idea that we need to dispense with everything we think we own is a common one and what is forgotten is that the core possession is the sense of a separate self. In other words, if you decide that liberation means dispensing with everything, make sure you dispense with your life as well:

"Some people will hear the words, 'Nothing is mine' and they will get the idea they should throw away all their possessions. With only superficial understanding, people will get into arguments about what this means and how to apply it. But this is something to contemplate carefully. 'This is not my-self' doesn't mean you should end your life or throw away your possessions. It means you should give up attachment."

(Ajahn Chah: *Everything Arises, Everything Falls Away*)

The error is compounded if we go to the other extreme and justify the ownership of things by pretending that we have no attachments. Claiming that 'I have all these things, but I'm not really attached to them' is something that needs to be watched very carefully indeed!

Genuine surrender is what is really meant by 'giving no thought for the morrow'. It isn't a passive fatalism, but rather a conscious decision to relinquish attachments, to remain a passer-by. Conscious decisions require discriminating mind and only discriminating mind can reveal the measure of anything. For discriminating mind to function as it should, a prerequisite is acknowledging that nothing has any intrinsic value. The reason we go on thinking, looking, touching, eating, seeking, is that we've attributed value and meaning to thoughts and sense perceptions. And as Nisargadatta Maharaj reminds us, knowing that something has no intrinsic value doesn't necessarily mean not engaging in it. The choice to do so or not depends on a still, discriminating mind making the decision. Discipline is not denial and suffering, it is moving freely under the constraint of measure.

"Discrimination is the key. Through it, one can see one's own desires for things one lacks and one can also see that those who have the things one covets are not happy. Neither happiness nor misery dwell in things, but in one's own decision, made through discrimination."

(Shantanand Saraswati: *Good Company*)

A measured life means making choices about how we act, such as the choice to not feed a craving. We must act – even not acting is an action – but the important question is, how shall we act? Buddhists describe it as a paradox: there's no going forward, no going back and you can't stay in the same place. The paradox of acting but not acting is resolved by discovering what it is that acts. Body and mind act, Self just observes, hence the Vedic injunction, 'in truth, I do nothing at all'. The mistaken identity of what I am (consciousness) with what I am not (some physical form or thought) intervenes in the process of choice and obscures discriminating mind. So what is conscious choice? We think of ourselves as having the freedom to choose, but how free are we?

The idea of having choice is embedded in our language: 'I had no choice but to…' or 'what choice have I got?' and advertisers tell you that 'It's your choice'. What advertisers intend to convey is that the only real choice is to buy their product. We decide to buy a particular model of car and the salesperson assures that it was 'a wise choice', which probably means we've been persuaded to buy the most expensive model. Ego loves to hear how wise, wonderful and beautiful it is, which will certainly help to clinch the deal. Most of the choices we speak about are relative ones, between one kind of coffee and another, between marrying someone or not marrying them, about divorcing from someone or not divorcing. None of these things – coffee, marriage, divorce, cars – has any intrinsic value or meaning, so we're struggling to choose between valueless things. Nonetheless, making choices is a constant in our daily lives, so how do we make choices that are wise?

A useful starting point is to remind ourselves that in pure consciousness, there is no choice to be made; consciousness is one, with no separate things to choose between and no separate chooser. However, we exist as forms in the relative world, where choices are made between two or more things, and discriminating mind is what choice revolves around. The ordinary choices we make in the world need to be taken from the detached third point afforded by discriminating mind.

We might be determined always to take the cheapest option irrespective of how much money we have, which is likely to be as ignorant an action as insisting on always having the most expensive (justified by phrases like, 'you get what you pay for', or 'it was money well spent'). Closer examination generally shows that emotion is what governs most of the choices we make, rather than reason. There isn't anything wrong with emotion, but it does act as the glue that makes the bond of attachment so difficult to surrender. Let's return to our earlier example of traffic lights to provide a simple, practical way of bringing together the principles of Enlightened Living as well as illustrating choice and how it can be compromised by emotion. The lights change according to measure – if you wait long enough at a red light it will turn green. This is an explicit, planned form of measure, but measure nonetheless. When the light changes the traffic moves in one direction and stops in another, which is cause and effect. Red lights cause stopping, green lights cause moving and we stop at red lights and go for green lights as a result of conditioning.

So, what happens when you approach a controlled intersection? Suppose the light has been green for a while. There is still a car in front of you when the light changes to amber. What arises in your mind and how do you act? Do you desperately squeeze in behind the last car to get through? Or you've been in the traffic queue for a while and as you move forward on green the driver at the front hesitates about going through. What do you do? And what do you do when you find yourself waiting in a slow queue? Ego is about justifying rather than examining and when thoughts arise at traffic lights of the 'come on, come on!!' variety, they'll usually be justified by how you need to get to the shop you're heading for and here's this person having the gall to hold you up. We really do believe the queue is put there to prevent the world being the way this amazingly important and famous person wants it to be. Little wonder that road rage occurs.

All this is living a justified life, so here's the alternative way of living an examined life. Traffic lights change at regular intervals. When they turn green, the queue in front of you will move, according to measure. If someone goes through slowly, they go through slowly. If the light changes again (and again and again) before you get your turn, all that means is that they change again (and again and again) before you get your turn. If you're going to be late for a meeting, you're going to be late for a meeting. Putting a full stop at the end of each sentence means just that: full stop. There's nothing more to add, other than the trumpeting of ego. Everything is subject to cause and effect, which is neutral. Where are you rushing off to? Death, actually, since that's the destination of every creature.

In these situations emotion arises, as it will; the question is where it goes from there. Choosing wisely in the relative world means being able to acknowledge conditioning, surrender attachments and act according to the need, using uncontaminated discriminating mind. The choices we make may begin innocuously enough as simple conditioning – we're conditioned to recognise what to do when traffic lights are red or green – but all too often they end in attachment. The choice is whether you live a justified life or an examined one. Fed by desire and aversion we develop preferences, but there can be a very short step from preference to addiction.

What renders us unable to respond with 'Is that so?' is fame. Fear of being taken advantage of or made to look foolish, which is fame. Desperation to win whatever issue is at hand, which is fame. Saying how useless we are, or how miserable we feel, which is fame. We can be famous heroes as much as famous victims. Examining these attachments doesn't mean analysing them and picking them apart and even less so criticising yourself for developing the attachment. Because nothing has intrinsic value or meaning there's nothing personal – 'personal' is the view from ego and invites justification.

Making something personal is a choice based on separation and leads to ignorance like road rage, but the person in whom it is all vested, ego, only exists as attachments. Everything in the relative world is a temporary state of mind or matter that comes into being exists for a while and then ceases to exist. The mistake is to want to defy measure and to make them certain and permanent:

"All beings, including humans, tend to see the arising as themselves, the existence as themselves and the cessation as themselves. Thus they cling to everything. Having experienced happiness, they don't want suffering. If suffering does arise, they want it to go away as quickly as possible. But it is even better if it doesn't arise at all. This is because they see this body and mind as themselves, or belonging to themselves, so they demand those things to follow their wishes."

(Ajahn Chah: *Food for the Heart*)

This desire for things to remain the same forever, to be certain and controllable, is to work against measure. Measure is maintained by the opposite, by surrender. We've been conditioned to see surrender as negative, giving up when we should be fighting on, standing up for our rights, opposing evil, etc. etc. Enlightened Living does not say that evil should be cultivated, or that we shouldn't speak out if we see an injustice, but we need to do so from an indifferent perspective. Most of our thinking about what is good and evil is relative and defined by ego. Surrender doesn't mean that action stops, but it does mean that identification with being the doer of actions stops.

The tendency to want good rather than evil is praiseworthy, as is the preference to want to be happy rather than unhappy. However, the extremes of good and evil, happiness and unhappiness are relative states and to be really free is to transcend them both. This is the conundrum we're faced with: we ordinarily think that we have to be in one or other state. When the wise sit, they just sit. 'Just sitting' doesn't mean asleep and half-dead, or not acting when action is required. It means resting in the present, acting only when there is something in the present to be attended to and surrendering the idea that I'm the doer of actions. A Zen story describes how Bankei responded to claims for mystical powers by a priest in the audience:

"'The founder of our sect,' boasted the priest, 'had such miraculous powers that he held a brush in his hand on one bank of the river, his attendant held up a paper on the other bank and the teacher wrote the holy name of Amida through the air. Can you do such a wonderful thing?'

Bankei replied lightly: 'Perhaps your fox can perform that trick, but that is not the matter of Zen. My miracle is that when I feel hungry I eat and when I feel thirsty I drink.'"

(Paul Reps: *Zen Flesh, Zen Bones*)

Enlightenment is ordinary, ignorance is extraordinary. Isn't it extraordinary that we go on believing what ego tells us, despite the repeated veering from happiness to misery that it brings? When measure is followed without trying to control and change the universe, life becomes the natural and simple process that it is. For most of the time, we act in a state that is little different from sleep and completely subject to conditioning and attachment. Real choice enters when we acknowledge conditioning as a simple consequence of cause and effect, surrender attachments and meet the need.

This is a practical rather than a theoretical endeavour and as we saw in Chapter 3, one of the most useful ways of learning about measure and choice is to listen to our own speech. What will often happen when we do observe speech is discovering how much of it is redundant, so we're likely to say a lot less! As Epictetus noted, 'We have two ears and one mouth so that we can listen twice as much as we speak.' Measure and conscious choice are a consequence of clear discriminating mind and what obscures it are the attachments we become entangled by. We are free to choose, but that freedom only becomes available with enlightenment, when conditioning is acknowledged and attachments surrendered.

Chapter 9
Love and Reason

Gaining peoples' allegiance is described as winning their hearts and minds. Gaining allegiance has nothing to do with Enlightened Living, but the adage acknowledges the need to appeal to both love and reason. They are experienced as separate, even associated with different parts of our bodies and we do tend to be drawn by our individual conditioned natures towards one or the other. In this chapter, we'll draw a distinction between love and reason, often associated with 'heart' and 'head', respectively. They can both be subject to observation and are part of the relative world, but both also provide a path from relative to absolute; indeed, as we shall see, they merge in enlightenment.

We noted in Chapter 8 that love is conventionally seen as one of the emotions, along with anger, jealousy, guilt and the rest, but perhaps love ought not to be thought of as an emotion at all. What we describe as emotions are passing states, as ephemeral as mirages. Once we identify with them they become the lifeblood of attachments, justified in our minds by invoking ego: we claim to be justifiably angry when the car in front is slow going through the traffic light. We all feel frustration or even anger arising from time to time, but provided it isn't indulged it can be surrendered and allowed to pass. In the previous chapter we emphasised that there's nothing wrong with emotion, but it becomes an obstacle to enlightenment when it dictates our lives: emotion is what keeps addictions going. If an emotion like anger is an often-repeated habitual response, it might be time to ask yourself why you're always so angry, rather than justifying it.

Emotion gives a particular quality or tone to the thoughts that arise in our minds – it confers a value on them, positive or negative. These value-laden attributions are held in the function of mind we described in Chapter 3 as conserving mind and through conditioning they become entrenched. Up to this point, they can usefully help to guide our responses, but without mindful practice they can become automatic and habitual rather than spontaneous. The real problem, however, is when they're fed and nurtured as attachments and we're less and less able to detach ourselves from them. We often speak of treasuring our memories, but we need to be mindful of what we treasure:

"A good man out of the good treasure of the heart bringeth forth good things: and an evil man out of the evil treasure bringeth forth evil things."

(*Matthew 12:36*)

What are 'bad' and 'good' things? In Chapter 1 we used the example of how we might respond to beggars to illustrate the practise of observing our minds. One person might not give because they think the money will be spent on drugs, or might studiously ignore them, perhaps even crossing the road to avoid the encounter altogether. The next person stops and gives the beggar money. Conventionally, the first person would be thought of as uncharitable and mean – bad – while the second would be considered good. But what if the second person walked away with self-righteous feelings of pride in their good-heartedness? Both of these states of mind result in an equal degree of separateness.

The resolution is in both cases to surrender the fruit of the actions. An indifferent person treasures nothing. Whatever arises in the mind, bring it under observation, surrender the attachments that arise and act from the detached third point of discriminating mind. What might then happen can't be prescribed. You may or may not give to the beggar: your actions are an effect and what counts is the cause of the action. What is surrendered is the justification of actions based on ego. Justifying consolidates attachments; examining in the light of discriminating mind dissolves them. What confers the very different feelings experienced by the two people in our example is emotion and emotions will continue to arise, but with detachment, they can be seen as passing states having no intrinsic value.

The same is true for the ordinary sense in which we describe love. When we fall in love with someone our minds become filled with thoughts about that person, to the point of distraction. We're desperate to see them again and when we're apart the desperation grows with each passing day; we miss them with what feels like a physical ache. We proclaim we'll love them forever and the craving continues until they eventually become part of the furniture and we 'fall out of love' with them. It can even turn to loathing and jealousy. So what was this 'love'? It seems more a temporary addiction to a sentimental attachment, fuelled by a passing emotion. What we suggested in Chapter 8 is a different way of thinking about love, not as a passing emotional state but as the very quality of consciousness. And here's where language trips us up: we're using the same word to describe a passing state on the one hand, while at the same time saying it is absolute. How can we draw a distinction between these 'loves'?

Emotions are often described using our bodies as a reference point. Fear, for example, is like a 'knot in the stomach', rage is a red mist that rises and blinds us and when someone leaves us we are broken-hearted. Although some bodily changes might be specific to particular emotions, these links to parts of the body are largely metaphorical. What is common to all of them and what locates them firmly in the relative world, is separation. This is obvious with anger or fear or jealousy but is equally true with ordinary love. We might want to become one with the person we love, but for as long as this love is thought about in relative terms it can never happen: bodies and minds *are* separate.

Looked at objectively, you probably fell in love with this other person because their particular conditioning and attachments happen to mesh rather well with your own. This is the extent of supposedly 'being made for each other'. What it actually is, is chance: a haphazard meeting of complementary egos. Since this relative love is all about ego it can be a very dark place indeed, as evidenced by what happens when that same love is transformed into hatred: a significant proportion of murders are committed by spurned partners or ex-lovers, fuelled by anger and jealousy.

Describing relative love in this way isn't an encouragement to love no one and those who profess to love no one probably remain very much in love with the person proclaiming it! Even though relative love and loathing are merely passing states, the difference between them is that the first is far less likely to cause harm than the second, so in a relative sense it is certainly better to love than to hate. Unfortunately, however, they're rather like two sides of the same coin.

Love in the relative world involves two people and what you love is in part the very thing that makes them different from you – the physical form, for example. You're also, of course, attracted to things about the person that are similar to you, but the love is between two separate forms. We might try to cultivate a love for everyone through compassion, but the literal meaning of the word is 'suffering together'. That can easily become sympathy: if you identify with the misery that someone else is experiencing, you just end up with two people suffering. This is an obstacle to meeting the need. After all, doctors don't need to suffer from the same diseases as their patients to be able to help them. What they do need is to understand that their patient *is* suffering, but not to take on the suffering themselves. What's required and not just in the context of doctors and their patients, is a detached form of compassion, best described as empathy rather than sympathy.

Love will arise, but what will prevent it from becoming attachment is indifference. Absolute love is the very nature of consciousness and is never absent and neither is it affected by changes in the relative world. Indifferent love means continuing to love, come what may. Although the fundamental nature of bodies and minds prevails, the forms themselves alter over time: attitudes change and bodies age. That's what the world of forms is about, but despite the uniqueness of each form and the changes they undergo, they remain forms of the same single consciousness. It is this that is forgotten or ignored.

Acknowledging consciousness allows relative love to be seen for the passing state that it is. After all, you and the other will both die, whether or not you continue to feel the emotional attraction until that happens. What can be known simultaneously is that you are both forms of the same consciousness: from this perspective you are indeed one. Swami Vivekananda expressed this poetically in his Teachings:

"We all begin with love for ourselves and the unfair claims of the little self make even love selfish; at last, however, comes the full blaze of light, in which this little self is seen to have

become one with the Infinite. Man himself is transfigured in the presence of this Light of Love and he realises, at last, the beautiful and inspiring truth that Love, the Lover and the Beloved are one."

(Swami Vivekananda: *Teachings of Swami Vivekananda*)

As we've already said, consciousness isn't a perceptible entity. All that you can be aware of is its reflection in the form of attention. To really love someone is to recognise relative and absolute simultaneously: attraction to the passing form, while at the same time acknowledging that it is a form of the same consciousness that is your own Self. It is a love which transcends the inevitable changes in the form that time wreaks; indeed, it is something which exists independently of the forms altogether. What the forms experience is a reflection of this love, in just the same way that consciousness is reflected as attention through the forms. This is the love Shakespeare describes:

"Let me not to the marriage of true minds
Admit impediments. Love is not love
Which alters when it alteration finds,
Or bends with the remover to remove:
Oh no! it is an ever-fixed mark,
That looks on tempests and is never shaken;
It is the star to every wandering bark,
Whose worth's unknown, although his height be taken?
Love's not Time's fool, though rosy lips and cheeks
Within his bending sickle's compass come;
Love alters not with the brief hours and weeks,
But bears it out even to the edge of doom.
If this be error, and upon me prov'd,
I never writ, nor no man ever loved."

(William Shakespeare: *Sonnet 116*)

Consider what he means in the poem. This love simply doesn't change, come what may and it lasts 'even to edge of doom'. In other words, it is eternal and exists irrespective of the forms that come and go. This is how we might describe consciousness, so love is indistinguishable from consciousness. To be in this love is to be one's own self, which is also what happens in deep meditation: separation disappears. Absolute love doesn't require an object to invest it in – whether or not there is another being makes no difference.

The love of another person often starts with physical attraction, which is why ordinary love is so often confounded with sex. What we desire in another form is largely a convention, but we become bound by it: our partner ages and they're no longer as beautiful or handsome as we once thought they were and the supposedly undying love we promised them suddenly fades. Perhaps their desire for sex has diminished and the same thing happens. The poem describes a different love, one that endures when lips and cheeks are less rosy than they once were. Sex is also why we're conditioned to think of love as exciting, but bliss and excitement are in fact mutually exclusive.

There are and will continue to be separate forms, but we need not become attached to them or identified with them. Experiencing unity rather than separation, all of the judgements based on difference disappear:

"In love, you always give and don't demand in return. By giving, you allow things to happen. When people love someone, they forget that real love means no demands from the beloved."

(Shantanand Saraswati: *Good Company*)

From the perspective of Enlightened Living, love is paradoxically indifferent, and it isn't something that is given from one to another. There isn't a store of it to be released to some but withheld from others – it isn't selective. All that's required for absolute love to manifest is to surrender the separation that comes from attachment, which we illustrated in Chapter 5 with the metaphor of the trough of water with a barrier inserted into it. Where there appeared to be two separate bodies of water when the barrier is removed there is just one.

Relative love is one among many emotions, fleeting states of mind that come and go. It may change over time and is selective, given to some but not to others. There is also something in it for the participants, loving or being loved. Absolute love is not one among many different changeable states. It is synonymous with consciousness and is ever-present, obscured only by the attachments of ego. Being in the world means that there are particular people to whom we devote the relative emotional feeling of love, but that's not inconsistent with also being able to acknowledge consciousness in everyone, or indeed in every form. When Jesus speaks of loving thy neighbour as thyself he doesn't mean to have the same literal relative love for everyone. He himself apparently favoured one particular disciple and expressed little love for the scribes and Pharisees, but that doesn't preclude the Herodians saying of him that 'thou art true and carest for no man: for though regardest, not the person on men' (The Gospel According to Mark, 12: 14). The 'person of men' are the passing states of their relative forms, which may not be lovable at all, as every parent knows: you love your children, but may not always love the way they behave!

Perhaps this helps us make sense of what Jesus says to his disciples in the Gospel of Thomas:

> (Logion 13) "Make a comparison to me and
> tell Me whom I am like."
> Simon Peter said to Him: "Thou art like a
> righteous angel."
> Matthew said to Him: "Thou art like a wise man of understanding."
> Thomas said to Him: "Master, my mouth will not at all be capable of saying whom Thou art like."
> Jesus said: "I am not thy Master because thou hast drunk
> from the bubbling spring which I have measured out."
>
> (*The Gospel of Thomas*)

Thomas knows that consciousness can't be described, and what he acknowledged was not the person of Jesus but the Self. This is enlightenment and Thomas no longer had any need for a master to point the way. Jesus was a man, replete with all of the usual conditioning. Relatively free of attachments, to be sure, but just a man, different in form from all other conditioned forms. What Thomas knew but couldn't put into words or concepts is that the form was at the same time a form of a single consciousness.

The love being described here is indifferent and is thus not conditioned by personal differences – it is unconditional. The idea of unconditional love is a familiar one, trotted out as the key to happy relationships. Practising it is another matter. It requires the first principle of this teaching, which is that everything is a form of consciousness. Could you love a paedophile? Hitler? Their behaviour is not what is loved; what is loved is Self and they are forms of the same unchanging consciousness as your own self. In the Old Testament this unified love is described as charity:

"Charity suffereth long and is kind; charity envieth not; charity vaunteth, not itself, is not puffed up,

Doth not behave itself unseemly, seeketh not her own, is not easily provoked, thinketh no evil;

Rejoiceth not in iniquity, but rejoiceth in the truth;

Beareth all things, believeth all things, hopeth all things, endureth all things.

Charity never faileth: but whether there be prophecies, they shall fail; whether there be tongues, they shall cease; whether there be knowledge, it shall vanish away."

(*1 Corinthians 13:4–8*)

Indifferent love should not be taken to mean that you love the way ego behaves, or that you don't have compassion for the suffering of others. While it is true that suffering is a consequence of ego and is ignorant in the sense that the word is used in Enlightened Living – to ignore the consciousness that unifies all forms – to tell someone who is suffering that they're ignorant is in itself judgemental and egoistic and is certainly not meeting the need:

Q: So one should try to ameliorate suffering, even if one knows that ultimately it is non-existent?

A: *"There never was and never will be a time when all are equally happy or rich or wise or healthy. In fact, none of these terms has any meaning except in so far as the opposite to it exists. But that does not mean that when you come across anyone who is less happy or more miserable than yourself, you are not to be moved to compassion or to seek to relieve him as best you can. On the contrary, you must love all and help all, since only in that way can you help yourself. When you seek to reduce the suffering of any fellow man or fellow creature, whether you succeed or not, you are yourself evolving spiritually if the service is rendered disinterestedly, not within the egotistic feeling 'I am doing this'."*

(Godman (Ed): *Be as You Are – The Teachings of Ramana Maharshi*)

The key is in Ramana Maharshi's final sentence: 'if the service is rendered disinterestedly'. Any action can be performed with or without the claim of being the agent or actor. When an action is indifferent, you as a separate individual who does things and then claims the fruit of the action has been removed and consciousness flows unimpeded. This is what we meant earlier by 'detached compassion' and is what Jesus meant in the Gospel of Thomas as being a 'passer-by': not someone who does nothing, just walks past someone suffering and ignores them, but rather in offering help to that person, does so with no expectation of personal gain from it.

If love is associated with heart, reason is associated with head or mind. Love and reason are usually juxtaposed. When someone becomes overwhelmed by emotion, we appeal to them to 'just be reasonable' and if they lack compassion they're judged heartless. Head and heart are often distinguished by the temperature ascribed to them; usually warm heart, cold reason. What we associate with heart is emotion, while head functions with emotionless logic. In fact, they are both functions of mind and although the different functions often act in concert and can hardly be separated from one another, in Chapter 3 we distinguished between the two functions associated with heart and head: emotional mind and discriminating mind.

We've drawn a clear distinction in this chapter between the ordinary experience of love, which is attachment and the love that arises when the unity of the Self is acknowledged. Much the same can be said for reason, since it operates at both relative and absolute levels. Discrimination is always between two or more things, so it governs choice: choosing a chocolate flavoured ice-cream instead of a vanilla one, for example. As we saw in Chapter 7, we imagine we have free will to choose, but why do we choose the chocolate ice-cream rather than vanilla? Because we've had chocolate and vanilla ice creams before and we preferred chocolate – in other words, we've become conditioned and our conditioning governs the choices we make. But what happens when we've been standing for a long time in a queue for an ice-cream and the person in front of us is served the last scoop of chocolate? It is easy to see how innocuous conditioning can become an attachment and that's when it becomes a problem: what appears as choice has been coloured by ego.

It is possible to exercise free choice, but only when the choice is a conscious one, rather than a mechanical one performed in waking sleep. This is easy to practise by watching what it is that's governing the choices we make and since we're making choices all the time there are ample opportunities. We might try to free ourselves from the dilemma by refusing both chocolate and vanilla ice-cream, but that too is a choice and we end up not being able to enjoy either! It doesn't actually matter which you choose and the conditioning that leads to preferring chocolate isn't the issue. The question is whether you're aware of what determines the choice you make.

Using discriminating mind to choose between flavours happens in the relative world, but discriminating mind also knows the difference between what is relative and what isn't. This is pure reason, though just as with love, much of what passes for reason in ordinary language is simply ego at work. When we ask people to just be reasonable, what we actually mean is, just agree with me! Pure reason can only really happen when it isn't filtered through ego.

For love or reason to be indifferent requires surrender of the attachments that bind both the head and the heart. It doesn't necessarily require giving anything away, but rather realising that everything is a form of consciousness and that that consciousness is love:

"To realise this it is neither necessary to resign your job nor run away from home. Renunciation does not imply apparent divesting of costumes, family ties, home etc., but renunciation of desires, affection and attachment. One who renounces desires actually merges in the world and expands his love to the whole universe. Expansion of love would be a far better term for a true devotee than renunciation. A sannyasi who apparently casts away his clothes and leaves his home does not do so out of

aversion to his relations but because of the expansion of his love to others around him. When this expansion comes, one does not feel that one is running away from home, instead one drops from it like a ripe fruit from a tree. Till then it would be folly to leave one's home or job."

(Godman (Ed): *Be as You Are – The Teachings of Ramana Maharshi*)

Even the title of the book from which this quote is taken emphasises what Shakespeare described as the readiness being all: be as you are and when the measure we described in Chapter 7 has been fulfilled the ripe fruit will drop, not before.

In the Vedic tradition, the different paths to enlightenment are described as yogas. The root of the English word 'yoke' is yoga, in other words linking yourself to a teaching. Being yoked conjures up associations of oxen yoked to plough and it seems the opposite of being free, but the yoke of yoga is the discipline that allows you to move freely. Exactly the same idea is expressed in the Christian teaching:

"Come unto me, all ye that labour and are heavy laden and I will give you rest.

Take my yoke upon you and learn of me; for I am meek and lowly in heart: and ye shall find rest unto your souls.

For my yoke is easy and my burden is light."

(*Matthew 11:28–30*)

Two of the Vedic paths to enlightenment correspond directly to heart and head: *bhakti yoga* – the path of love and devotion – and *jnana yoga*, or the path of pure reason. There is no doubt that our conditioned nature will lead us more towards one path than another, which we described in Chapter 1 as being faced with many taxis when you want to go home. Each one might take a different route and by analogy, there are many paths on offer. Because of differences in our nature, some people might more easily be able to follow one rather than another, but it would be wrong to see them as leading to different ends: there aren't different kinds of enlightenment. With enlightenment, the differences in form, mind, and nature disappear, but nature, like body and mind, is an instrument that can be used in one of two ways: for ignorance or truth. If our nature draws us exclusively into relying on reason we may indeed become cold and if our nature is devotion we may be misled by blind faith.

Shantanand Saraswati describes how they can be reconciled:

"The stream of love and truth is one, but man catches it in two different ways, by heart or by mind. By heart he means his love, by mind he means his knowledge. But in fact, the stream of love and truth is always the same. Love and knowledge are the same thing but the function of love is to join together and that of knowledge to tell, to illuminate. In love, knowledge is helpful. For strengthening knowledge, love is essential. In the absence of love, knowledge would not be powerful enough to influence people. Knowledge only helps us to decide what is right and wrong, but it cannot alter things; love can alter them. Without love, knowledge is incomplete because, in the absence of knowledge, love would go away. If there is knowledge, then love is maintained. As love increases, knowledge also goes on increasing. Without knowledge, love is not expansive; and without love, knowledge is not allowed to play its full part."

(Shantanand Saraswati: *Good Company*)

Another great teacher from the Vedic tradition, Swami Vivekananda, expressed it in much the same way:

"There is not really so much difference between knowledge (Jnana) and love (Bhakti) as people sometimes imagine...in the end they converge and meet at the same point."

(Swami Vivekananda: *Bhakti Yoga*)

What Shantanand Saraswati and Swami Vivekananda are saying is that the two paths, sometimes described as separate, are in fact one and their end is enlightenment. Both involve surrender, ultimately the surrender of being a separate individual. Separation generates vested interests, but there is nothing for anyone to gain from enlightenment.

Chapter 10

Being in the World: Practising Enlightened Living

To recap briefly, the Enlightened Living teaching described in this book distinguishes between two 'realms', relative and absolute, but they are separated in this way purely for the purposes of description – all of the forms that constitute the relative world, whether they are physical entities or subtle thoughts, are forms of absolute consciousness. Unlike consciousness, the forms are temporary; they emerge, exist for a while and then pass. The physical forms can be known using our senses and we can also be aware of thoughts in our minds. Consciousness itself can't be known using senses and mind, but what we experience as awareness or attention is a reflection of consciousness through our bodies and minds. The attention we gave as children is no different from the attention we give as adults. How we interpret what we perceive will be very different, owing to differences in the conditioning that each of us has been exposed to, but attention is the same and is the same from one sentient creature to another.

Conditioning may be programmed by genetics or by learning, and is two-edged: on the one hand, it allows us to recognise and make sense of the world, but on the other, it can mean taking what we see for granted. Worse still, conditioning might be transformed into attachment. Attachment is the distortion of perception by ego, which separates the world into you as opposed to me. You and I have different forms of body and mind, but what is forgotten when ego takes over is that these are forms of a single consciousness. This is why ego is the source of all of the misery in the world and why enlightenment is no more or less than the dissolution of ego by surrendering attachments.

A key principle of Enlightened Living is that no form has any intrinsic meaning or value. Everything arises, lasts for a while, then ceases. That's what the relative world is, a sequence of forms endlessly transforming, governed by the law of cause and effect. There is no point or destiny involved – the only meaning or value in anything has been added to it, through our preference for some things and dislike of other things. However, to repeat a consistent message of Enlightened Living, this is not an invitation to do whatever you want or to just give up altogether. The truth is that consciousness is indifferent to even the most appalling thoughts you might nurture in your mind, but thinking in this way will often lead to acting accordingly. Ego has then taken a terrible form and suffering will undoubtedly ensue.

Mind is the battlefield: whatever arises there needs to be kept under observation, so that it can be seen for what it is and surrendered. When we let go of attachments, all that remains is consciousness. This is the paradox of enlightenment: we want to achieve things for me, but this 'me' is what goes when we become passers-by, simply responding to whatever need arises and based on the judgement of a clear discriminating mind. There is nothing for 'me' in enlightenment.

We've described the practice of Enlightened Living as being in the world but not of the world and the world is the relative realm of forms. We have no choice but to live our lives in it and the challenge is to do so without being beguiled by the endless temptations it offers. The dilemma is not resolved by rejecting the world – the Isha Upanishad we quoted from in Chapter 4 is emphatic in saying that the world is there to be enjoyed. What has hopefully become clear in this book is that living in an enlightened way is to enjoy without becoming attached, which is the focus of this final chapter.

For most of us, the trajectory of life begins with being cared for as infants, usually by one or two parents and maybe other kin. We then spend much of our childhood and adolescence at school, preparing for the adult world of work and relationships, perhaps also marriage and parenthood. We then enter retirement, a phase which can now last for 20 years or more. Then we die and the question posed by Enlightened Living is what we will do with this life, between being born and dying. Anyone reading this will already be at some point along the way and whatever part of the life already passed is now just a thought. The question is actually what we will do between *now* and dying and since we have no idea when we will die this is not a question that can be postponed – enlightenment isn't something you might think about taking up tomorrow, like golf or pottery.

The encouraging part, though, is that it doesn't require long preparation. You can be here now immediately, just by connecting with your senses and surrendering any attachments you can observe in the moment. From then on, all that's required to sustain mindfulness is maintaining observation as constantly as possible. Easier said than done, you might say, but we need to be wary of self-defeating comments. Yes, our minds will constantly be seeking novelty and stimulation and yes, attention will become captured, but to realise this you must already have stepped back and observed it. The period that your attention was captured must by definition have been in the past and what happened, even 10 seconds ago, is now no more than a thought. Just keep going, never mind the seeming 'failures' along the way.

Further help with observation and surrender comes from understanding that nothing has any intrinsic value or meaning, other than the value or meaning we attribute to it. If you have a car you might be able to see it objectively, as a manufactured form designed to get you from A to B. It does, of course, need to be looked after if it is to last, but that's different from the emotional investment in *my* car, which leads me to boast about it if it's expensive enough or to be devastated if it is damaged or stolen. Looking after it means repairing it when it is damaged, but it is just a car. The problem is compounded when it isn't an inanimate object. Then it becomes *my* wife/husband/partner, *my* children, with an emotional involvement far greater than anything evoked by a car.

Attachments are the source of our misery. How many of us are really happy at work? For many, it feels like something that cheats us out of 'our' time. We work more or less grudgingly as a means to the end of having money to spend and we're caught by attachments either way: attached to holidays and weekends as much as we're attached to disliking work. Or we become attached to work, identified with our role in the company and investing it with value and meaning it doesn't possess. It is difficult to account for the unexpected increase in death rates immediately after retirement, particularly amongst men, other than the sense of a loss of meaning.

You might say that we need to be passionate about what we do and that certainly is true, but passion is not the same as attachment. The difficulty is that we tend to invoke the 'thinking in twos' we described in Chapter 5: you're either passionate or a half-dead automaton. As we said there, what could be more like a half-dead automaton than acting mindlessly on programmed conditioning and attachment? Paradoxically, enjoying what you do can be completely indifferent, which means seeing work as a need to be met and meeting it without laying siege to resisting work or being attached to it. Everything, including work, can be done mindfully, provided you avoid investing it with negative or positive values it doesn't possess.

And marriage? In most Western countries marriage is based on sentimental emotion, a 'love' that often alters when it alteration finds. Few can see beyond the form, so it is little wonder that around 60% of marriages end in divorce. Instead of helping to forge an understanding of the world, most of the families we find ourselves in are a breeding ground for attachments and ignorance. The quote from Ajahn Chah in Chapter 5 captures this perfectly:

"Our parents teach us grasping and attachment, giving meaning to things, believing that we exist as a self-entity and that things belong to us. We hear this over and over again, and it penetrates our hearts and stays there as our habitual feeling. We're taught to get things, to accumulate and hold on to them, to see them as important and as ours."

(Ajahn Chah: *Everything Arises, Everything Fall Away*)

Just as with work, the relationships we engage in can be enjoyed without attachment, provided we can dissolve the ego that claims them for our separate selves. We've been conditioned to expect that the more we own and the more we do the more fulfilled we'll be, literally filling the life full, but what we're filling it with has no meaning or value. We follow platitudes about travel broadening the mind, when in fact it narrows the mind: we drive through foreign countries where we don't speak the language and have no actual connection with anyone living there and all we're left with are more thoughts to become attached to, longing to visit again or wishing we lived there too.

This doesn't mean we shouldn't travel, but we should aim to do it, and everything else, as mindfully as we can: enjoy, but without attachment to that enjoyment. As we saw in Chapter 5, a fulfilled life is a life in which no claim is made on the forms that come and go. Ramana Maharshi went to the mountain called Arunachala, near Tiruvannamalai in India when he was just 16 or 17 years old and is said never to have travelled more than a few miles from his ashram there. For all our travelling, there are few of us whose lives are as fulfilled as his was, giving unstintingly with no expectation of any return.

Or we might devour books about enlightenment. The problem with reading about something is that it isn't the same as doing it. You can read any number of books about meditation, but until you actually sit down, close your eyes and focus your attention on breathing or a mantra or a single object it will remain a theoretical idea. There isn't anything wrong with reading about something or discussing it with others and Enlightened Living describes this process of gaining understanding as an essential first step, but it will only provide the signpost to the destination. Unlike destinations when you're travelling, the destination of enlightenment is here now, and the route is practice in the here and now. This is why you don't have to go anywhere. There is no more consciousness available in India than there is in your own room.

We do all have a different way of responding to the world and we need to find the way that allows us the easiest path, otherwise, resistance will creep in. Trying to find the right system to provide understanding is entirely appropriate, provided it doesn't just become a search for something that suits ego! It definitely shouldn't be a search for a 'guru'. We attribute nonsensical ideas like 'full realisation' to people regarded as gurus and hope that enlightenment will happen by osmosis if we can get near enough to them. This is a false hope and also isn't in the interests of the supposed guru. You already have the perfect teacher, in the form of discriminating mind described in Chapter 3 – all you need is trustworthy signposts and dedicated practice.

Enlightenment only happens by practising what you've understood, to find out whether or not it is true. The place to practice is mind. Mind is where both ignorance and enlightenment spring from, so a useful question we often ask in Enlightened Living meetings is, 'what's in your mind now?' Stopping and examining what's being held there is the first step towards surrender – you can't surrender anything you're not even aware of. When we do this, the aim is not to analyse what we find or to discover where the thoughts have come from. They just come and go and trying to understand thoughts by finding what caused them will just devolve into empty psychobabble and guesswork. Observing them is all that's required. When thoughts are clearly observed the cause will sometimes become apparent, but knowing the cause isn't really the goal.

Here's an example: someone in an Enlightened Living meeting responded to the question by describing how she had been cut off by another car swerving in front of her on her way to the meeting. She'd gesticulated and shouted, even though the other car had by this time disappeared. The indignant tone that she described arising in her mind is familiar to us all: 'Idiot! People are such damn bad drivers; they just don't care as long as they've got ahead in the queue!' Well, maybe this particular person was indeed an inconsiderate driver, not taking account of others on the road. Maybe they were distracted momentarily and didn't see an oncoming car until the last minute. But maybe the member of the group had herself been distracted and had slowed down to the point where she was holding up the queue.

What happens in these events is that we almost always take our own personal perspective and then try to find ways of justifying why we became angry. Whatever the cause of the incident, what matters is to notice when this justification is happening – in other words, to examine your own mind rather than justifying yourself. Telling stories afterwards about the sequence of events will nearly always involve justification, so instead, just describe what arose in your mind, without allowing ego to interpret it. Doing so will usually reveal the foolishness of shouting at an unknown driver who has already disappeared down the road. This is what the member of the group discovered and the detachment that the observation afforded her provided the opportunity to surrender her attachment to indignation and anger.

Another member of the group used a strategy of telling himself how silly he was being by entertaining these thoughts, which is a good idea provided it remains light-hearted, otherwise if you keep telling yourself off you might end up just feeling guilty for doing it! Guilt has to be about something you've done in the past, which no longer exists other than in your mind and all you learn from it is how to be miserable. Remember the thousand-year rule: even something that happened ten minutes ago might just as well have been a thousand years ago. If there was useful information in the event, trust your mind to remember it when needed; the more mindful you were at the time the more likely it is that you will remember. For the rest, just let go.

The problem with any practice is that it is so much easier when you're prompted, for example by being asked a question. That serves as the alarm that wakes you up, so remembering to stop and ask yourself 'what's in your mind now' needs either an internal alarm or a signal from outside. In Chapter 6 we used the example of setting a small alarm outside the room when you first try meditating. This external alarm takes away all of the concerns that arise in your mind about how long you've been sitting there, as well as providing a choice point at which you could decide either to stop or to continue. An internal mindfulness alarm is developed through conditioning: the more you act on remembering and actually surrender attachments, the more frequently it will happen.

Most of us when we're concentrating on something will become physically or mentally tired and need to stretch and move about for a bit. Instead of drifting off into the next task while you're stretching; just connect with your senses by closing your eyes and listening. When you start doing this there is often a secondary cascade of thoughts, trying to identify what you can hear and in the process ushering in yet more thoughts. You can't *not* identify what you hear – this too is a result of conditioning and to listen to each sound as if it was the first time you've heard it can just become an intellectual exercise. Instead, allow listening to happen, letting the associated thoughts pass by returning your attention to just listening. All the sounds come to you, so there's no effort required – in other words, try to *allow* listening, rather than *doing* listening.

Being mindful, as with all of the practices, only happens in the present. Allowing actions to unfold under mindful observation means not becoming entangled in thoughts about yourself and what you're doing, or worse still, what you were doing yesterday or might do tomorrow. This doesn't preclude planning or drawing on experience, but rather doing them without losing the perspective of the present. The easiest way to anchor attention in the present is to use the practice of connecting with your senses. They only work in the present, and hence just stopping and listening will connect you with the present. From the perspective of the present, we can then begin to observe how mechanicalness creeps into what we do.

For example, we get up and get ready to go to work by going through a ritual, often with our minds already at work or captured by what we were doing last night. This can even creep into meditation when we're supposed to be practising an explicit form of mindfulness. The old adage that 'when the wise sit, they just sit' can remain just a clever phrase, but we should practise it as much as we can: when you meditate, just meditate. Connecting in this way, observing your mind, allows you to discover what your mind is full of: either stories with ego as the central character or just filled with attention that remains in the present and isn't captured by what passes. A helpful practice used by another member of an Enlightened Living meeting was to remember the full stop: instead of continuing to add thought sentences and creating stories, stop at the end of the first one and just do whatever is required.

The point about meditation is that when you practice it, you're not of the world. You are physically there but you've removed your attention from it by closing your eyes and using a strategy like attending to breathing to provide a focus. It isn't about distracting yourself. Thoughts continue to arise, but rather than engaging with them you allow them to pass by taking attention back to the alternating in- and out-breaths. In deep meditation, the removal from the world is even more pronounced: you're no longer aware of existing as a separate being. I recall talking to someone who had used a particular meditation practice for many years but said she no longer meditated at all. She wasn't saying that it had no value, or that she had somehow progressed beyond all of that, but what she had discovered was that after the practice she felt separate from the world around her. This experience came from the subtle claim that had been made – it had become 'my meditation'.

What she was seeking to practise instead was the constant vigilance of mindfulness in the world. It is essential that the stillness that comes with meditation is taken back into the way we act in the world, but the actual process of meditation remains a cornerstone of Enlightened Living. The feeling of separateness that might arise following meditation is most likely some claim on the peace of the meditative practice as 'mine', in which case it has become personal and part of ego. As we've said before, since enlightenment is about removing yourself from the picture, there is nothing in it for anyone. What the Buddha meant by saying that meditation is for lying down, sitting, standing and walking is that whatever we do needs to be done as mindfully as possible, but informed by the practice of deep meditation that removes our sensory connection with the world.

The idea of constant mindfulness can easily be hijacked. Distance runners will often talk about getting into a meditative state when they're running, but they're unlikely to emerge enlightened. People will often say that exercise provides relief from stress, but if you go for a 10-mile run and spend the whole time preoccupied with negative thoughts, you might end up fit but you'll still be miserable. We come back to the question: what's your mind full of? If it continues to be filled with ruminating about emotional upset, you'll remain stressed. If it is filled with idle daydreams about what you might do next weekend, you might not be stressed but you're certainly absent. If your mind is filled with consciousness – attention – without becoming attached to any of the thoughts that arise, that's mindfulness. Going into the past or the future will happen, as a consequence of conditioning or conscious planning, but once attachment arises to what's remembered or anticipated, ego is back in charge. Exercise is undoubtedly good for the body and since being in the present is about connecting with your physical senses it is entirely appropriate to ensure that your body is healthy. The danger is always attachment. Competitive sport is about running faster or further and wanting to win, but it is just a game. Winning or losing are like happiness and unhappiness: win some, lose some, neither has any intrinsic value or meaning.

What we are working against in our practice is reducing the sense of being a doer of actions and so we need to begin from where we are by observing the doing. This is the easiest way to become aware of attachments. When we close our eyes and practice mindfulness, in that stillness we can observe body and mind and know that we are neither. We then open our eyes and the conditioned, conventional reality rushes back in. Body and mind can then end up as instruments of ego, striving to achieve something. Most of our doing has a goal, which we're pleased about when we achieve it and disappointed when we don't. As soon as you connect with the world you're aware of things that need to be done; the challenge is maintaining mindfulness, being in the world but not of the world.

Being of the world is having consciousness captured for ego's ends; being in the world but not of it is paradoxically doing without being the doer. Most people have had some experience of this 'doingless doing'. For example, we go into work one day and everything seems to run so smoothly there is hardly a sense of having to act at all to get everything done. The next day, doing the same job, we feel as if we're wading through treacle. Nothing in the world has changed; the most likely change is something having been taken on in the mind. We convince ourselves that someone else ought to be doing this particular job, why should we have to do it? It starts from there and ends up in a firestorm of resentment and effort. Household chores are an even clearer example: 'why should I be doing all the washing up?', or 'If I didn't do it no one else would bother.' In other words, poor me, angry me, put upon me. Does it really matter who does it? Victimhood is a state of mind. We end up feeling cheated out of 'my time' or 'my life', when none of it belongs to anyone.

Conditioning is habit, and habits can be very useful – imagine having to learn how to use a computer all over again every time you sat down at one. The cost of habitual behaviour is that it might not just be automatic but also mindless. Mindfulness prevents this from happening and acting in the world as mindfully as possible means that actions are examined and not just engaged in like an automaton. To be mindful you need to be awake, with your attention given intentionally to whatever is in front of you in the moment, but it is simply the case that there isn't anyone who is awake all of the time. As we said in Chapter 3, our minds need to be entertained. If you don't provide something for your mind to attend to it will move off into whatever takes it's fancy.

This 'waking sleep' is the same as daydreaming and it will continue to happen. What the practice of Enlightened Living leads to is being more awake more of the time – we find ourselves waking up more and more frequently and able to stay awake longer. So, whenever you do wake up, stay awake as long as you can. This isn't an exhausting hypervigilance – in fact, there's no effort required at all in allowing consciousness to flow unimpeded. What it means is staying connected with the present moment for as long as you can by connecting with your senses.

We've already acknowledged the challenge of putting the wake up alarm in place and this is where technology can come to our aid. People of a certain age are fond of criticising technology probably because of the irritation at having any 10-year old able to tell them what they're doing wrong with their mobile phone, but technology is like anything else: it is an instrument that you can use. It can, of course, take over – just as the instrument of mind can end up using you when it gets monopolised by ego, people can become so involved in technology it becomes an end in itself, which is also likely to be driven by ego. But it can be very effective for initiating mindfulness, for example, having one of the common apps on your phone which sounds a tone at random intervals. Each time you hear it, you're woken up. This isn't mindfulness, just the reminder to be mindful, but an invaluable reminder nonetheless. You might say that after a while you won't notice it anymore and that's certainly true – it doesn't entertain the mind anymore, which is why any tool needs to be capitalised on as much as possible after it is first introduced.

Once we have woken up, the opportunity is available to live a more examined life. Even with established practices, resistance can arise. We've all been through phases where we've not felt inclined to meditate and forcing yourself to do it in these circumstances will have the opposite effect, of making you want to do it even less. The time comes to meditate, but there's something else we just need to do first. The thing we then end up doing first takes so long it isn't worth meditating now, so we tell ourselves we'll just meditate for a bit longer tomorrow. Tomorrow comes and something else intrudes to make the practice even shorter than usual. Then ego really takes hold and all sorts of justifications are offered: 'I've probably done enough meditating to last me for years', 'I think I need a break, I'll start again next month', 'I don't think I'm really getting any benefit from it', etc. And meditating stops. Think how often you've met someone who 'used to meditate'.

Let's put this into perspective, using meditation as the example. Meditation has lapsed. Don't regret that: regrets about not having done it and planning to do it tomorrow are both equally pointless thoughts. You must have remembered meditation to have realised it had lapsed, and remembering is the first and most important step – until you're aware of something, there'll be no change. Your thoughts about meditation are strong, but not strong enough to overcome the resistance and when the memory does arise it usually comes couched in all of the rituals that have become associated with meditation: a particular time, a favourite chair, a particular room in which you meditate. You check your watch, 'wrong' time; and what's the point with all the noise in that room now the neighbours have started their extension? We'll feel quite pleased to have found an excuse and no meditation happens.

Next time the memory returns, try not thinking about the rituals. You might be reclining reading a book; just gently put the book down, close your eyes and start the practice. Never mind that you're supposed to be sitting upright so the chakras are aligned – hopefully, we put paid to all those distracting mystical notions in Chapter 6! Just make sure you can breathe easily and you're comfortable, irrespective of how you're sitting. Stay with the practice for as long as you can, and when you're ready to stop, just stop. Once you have stopped, be aware of the ideas that start to come back into your mind. Maybe go back to your book, which gives something to rest your attention on. Sitting meditation is the preferred strategy in Enlightened Living and to be able to remain in a comfortable position for the duration of established practice generally requires being upright and with feet flat on the floor, but you can return to that gradually.

Trying to overcome resistance by effort is fruitless. You're fighting against ego. The solution is surrendering what arises in the mind. This is not the surrender of giving up, just the surrender of attachments and once this happens the 'enemy' ego is not vanquished, it just disappears. It never had any substance to start with, just mistaken thoughts. When you do wake up and connect with the present, the mindfulness that follows allows the opportunity for an examined life and the resistance can be observed. This isn't a matter of analysing it, just being aware of it and how persistent it can be. This is the attachment that you can then surrender.

We've been using meditation as an illustrative example, but resistance occurs in all aspects of our lives. On closer examination it can be seen as resistance to the measure we described in Chapter 7, in other words, wanting the world and especially other people, always to be the way we want them to be. Measure is the duration of a form. Measure is observable, and it offers the opportunity for practice: there is no point in struggling against the measure of something, like trying to obliterate unwanted thoughts from your mind. The measured way is to surrender the thoughts, not being concerned that they will continue to return until their measure is fulfilled, but not entertaining them by feeding them with attention when they do recur. Measure manifests in every form, from thoughts entering your mind to the genetic determination of your height; as Jesus said, no amount of thinking about being taller will add anything to your stature. Battling with thoughts serves only to strengthen them; keep them under observation and they won't overwhelm you.

The difficulty with observation is that it can never be purely objective. What you observe is always changed or distorted as a consequence of conditioning and it represents your personal interpretation of the world. This is inevitable and trying to attain 'pure' objectivity will end up as an empty philosophical discourse. Other than in deep sleep or deep meditation, the truth is that the sense of a separate 'me' will be retained, however subtly. An exercise that demonstrates this principle is to just sit, without moving around or engaging in any of the ideas about how enlightened people would sit, then close your eyes and allow listening. The key word is 'allow'. Given time, the mind settles down and stillness increases, which is one reason for practising the exercise, but we retain that subtle sense of being the listener. This is ego, perhaps a fairly benign ego in these circumstances, but ego nonetheless: a separate 'me' doing the listening. The aim of practising Enlightened Living is to surrender as far as possible the attachment to that separate individual. In other words, to become nobody!

This is so difficult. Who wants to be nobody? The idea of being a nobody is usually framed as someone who is put upon by everyone else, has no opinions of their own, who achieves nothing. Maybe this person being described is all of these things as a consequence of their attachment to ego as a victim, but perhaps not. Of what value are people's opinions? The only achievements that people tend to value are fame and fortune, which neither matter nor have any intrinsic value. A true passer-by doesn't in any sense feel a victim; indeed, their sense of self is immeasurably strong because it is informed by a clear sense of Self. Practising humility isn't about abasing yourself – how could you abase Self? The way we can begin to become passers-by is by truly realising that none of the forms have any intrinsic value. The only value is what we attribute to them. Added to this, though, is that it isn't about rejecting everything, becoming cynically nihilistic or despondent. There's no need for despondency when everything, though having no intrinsic value, is a form of absolute consciousness. When cynicism and despondency take over, the heart is closed and the bliss that is everyone's birth right has been covered over.

'Opening the heart' is a common phrase and it does have a kind of intrinsic appeal that we can easily relate to, but how do we practice it? As we saw in Chapter 9, there are two ways of practising, through reason or through love, often described as head or heart. They are not exclusive and the quote we used from Shantanand Saraswati in that chapter emphasises that wisdom isn't about using one or the other but having both. Each of us does tend to have a nature that will predispose us towards one or the other, which carries risks: working exclusively from reason can omit compassion and working from love can incur overwhelming emotion or blind faith. Faith is a belief in something in the absence of evidence. The evidence we need is available through observation, judged with an open heart and a clear discriminating mind.

Notice the effect on us of hearing people speaking about their emotions: does your mind tend to respond with thinking they ought to 'get a grip'? And if we hear an emphasis on thinking and logic, do we dismiss it as 'academic'? Reason is what characterises the process of understanding, using concepts to frame ideas and is an essential starting point. We need concepts to begin to understand the difference between the ordinary self of ego and Self of absolute consciousness, but in the absence of practice it won't go any further. To practice, the heart has to be open to whatever might arise, especially in one's own mind, without immediately justifying it.

An Enlightened Living principle is that there isn't anything personal. The feeling of personal or private automatically closes your heart. This doesn't mean disclosing all kinds of private things – that's the domain of psychotherapy. Expressing emotion in therapy is a way to help psychological healing, consolidating what might often be a fairly fragile sense of self; Enlightened Living is about dispensing with self. The practice is to observe, without judgement and the question is always the same: what was discovered? The reason why regular meetings with like-minded people are so important is that they provide the opportunity for speaking dispassionately about what has been observed, and when we speak about our observations we're describing situations where we've used our understanding in order to practice in the world.

A real opening of the heart happens when we 'see the Self in others'. We put this into perspective in Chapter 4: you can't see Self, only consciousness reflected as attention and trying to 'see' Self is nonsensical. The aim is to acknowledge that this consciousness or attention that you can be aware of, seemingly shining from another, is the same attention that lights your mind. Attention can be used to feed anything, from dark ignorance to unconditional love and you're likely to see the whole gamut when you observe mindfully – both in yourself and in the other. What you're observing is conditioning or the attached claim on the conditioning and since this happens for the other as much as it does for you, there is the opportunity to surrender judgements. This is what an open heart is: a non-judgemental acceptance of what you find and a unity rather than separation. Bodies and minds are all different; the consequence of thinking that you are just body and mind is that unity is impossible. The emotional experience that arises when criticism is suspended is love, not the attached love of selecting what you like or don't like, but the unconditional – in other words, without conditions – accepting of oneness despite outward differences.

The heart opens when the separate sense of self has been dissolved, but we need to be realistic in our expectations of this practice, otherwise, we might end up feeling disappointed when enlightenment proves elusive. We've already acknowledged how hard it is to remove ourselves from the scene and how easy it is for ego to reassert itself in our minds. Rather than creating an expectation of being completely free of ego, we begin to notice the changes that happen in our everyday lives as we become more mindful. People often link their unhappiness to feeling stressed, but without properly understanding that stress is not being able to surrender preoccupations with emotional upsets. Have you ever finished everything you've had to do at work? Occasionally maybe, but most people simply have too much to do. We so easily become fearful of what the consequences might be of not getting something done, but forgetting that we're all in the same boat – nobody always finishes everything on time. This is not to say we shouldn't try to do so, but becoming fearful or frustrated by the amount of work we have is pointless.

More importantly, our workload has nothing to do with stress. Workload is a demand to perform, which is pressure. There is a widely held view that there is 'good' and 'bad' stress and that a bit of stress is good for you, but if you ask people how they feel when they say they're stressed, the answer is likely to be some form of misery. Nothing that makes you miserable can possibly be good for you. What is useful is pressure, which is just a requirement to do something. It starts from the moment you wake up when the requirement is to get up. When you get to work, the pressure might increase, especially if something goes pear-shaped in your team! But no matter how intense the pressure, it isn't stress.

As the demand increases, so too do your heart rate and blood pressure, as a consequence of an increase in adrenaline. This fight-or-flight reaction is entirely appropriate: adrenaline gets you going, but contrary to popular belief it isn't a 'stress hormone', just a hormone doing exactly what it should be doing. The increase in cardiovascular strain isn't a problem, provided you can return to a resting level afterwards and allow your body to recover. Stress is when this isn't allowed to happen and adrenaline and another hormone secreted during fight-or-flight, called cortisol, are kept at unnaturally high levels. Adrenaline increases cardiovascular demand and if cortisol is sustained when it is no longer needed it can impair immune function.

There are very unusual circumstances which don't easily allow recovery, but for most of us the pressure we're under is not constant, it comes and goes. To turn pressure into stress, all you need do is to continue to ruminate about the frustrations, fears and other emotional upsets that might have arisen. This churning on about what-ifs and if-onlys serves no purpose whatsoever and is mostly imagined. To paraphrase Mark Twain, some of the worst things in our lives never happened. We try to fool ourselves that we're problem-solving with all this emotional churning, but we're not. An example: think back to the last time you had an argument with someone which you lost. What happens for the next days or weeks? Over and over in your mind, you end up winning! You lost; this serves no purpose except to retrieve something for 'me', to be somebody who always wins. When we get caught up in ruminating our minds fill up with thoughts about what-if and if-only, which is the same as worry – if you wanted a definition of worry, it would be something like ruminating about emotional upset. Once stress can be properly defined as ruminating or churning, we can see clearly how it prolongs the misery as well as making an unnatural demand on your body.

Ego is what gets upset about losing or crows when winning. Defining stress appropriately, as continuing to churn over issues that have happened in the past or might happen in the future, is what we mean by claiming the fruit of the action: becoming attached to the emotion evoked by these negative thoughts. The way to remove this separate self requires surrender and what needs to be surrendered is the attachment to the thoughts. This isn't about not doing anything. There are always needs to be met, but you can act in the world with or without the addition of negative thinking. We can then begin to see this as a choice and not something we're subjected to as victims of circumstance. The choice is either to continue to identify with the upset or to let it go. The easiest way to let it go is to return to the present moment and the easiest way to do that is to connect with your senses. What facilitates letting go is seeing all of the dramas and stories created in the mind as having no intrinsic meaning or value and having let go, instead of mind being filled with negative emotions it is filled instead with awareness. Whatever needs to be done will still be there waiting, but it can now be done mindfully.

The only alternative to mindfulness is to sleepwalk through life, endlessly finding ways to justify ourselves and endlessly procrastinating: 'I'll definitely start meditating tomorrow'. Remember the quote from Shakespeare's *Macbeth* in Chapter 5:

> "To-morrow, and to-morrow, and to-morrow,
> Creeps in this petty pace from day to day,
> To the last syllable of recorded time;
> And all our yesterdays have lighted fools
> The way to dusty death. Out, out, brief candle!
> Life's but a walking shadow, a poor player
> That struts and frets his hour upon the stage,
> And then is heard no more; it is a tale
> Told by an idiot, full of sound and fury,
> Signifying nothing."
>
> (William Shakespeare: *Macbeth, Act 5 scene V*)

Tomorrow and tomorrow: the seconds, minutes, hours, days, weeks and years tick by. Enlightenment is now, so the time to act is now.